CW01652988

LET ME PLAY THE LION, TOO

50 Years of Amateur Theatre in Bromley

by

Vicky Huntley

Bromley Theatre Guild

50th Anniversary
1949 – 1999

BROMLEY THEATRE GUILD

Copyright © 1999 Bromley Theatre Guild

First published in Great Britain in 1999 by Bromley Theatre Guild, 44 Hayes Road, Bromley, Kent, BR2 9AA.

All rights reserved. No part of this publication may be reproduced, stored in a retrieval system, or transmitted in any form or by any means, electronic, mechanical, photocopying, recording or otherwise, without written permission of Bromley Theatre Guild.

Designed and typeset by Paperweight

Printed in Great Britain by The Cromwell Press, Trowbridge, Wiltshire

ISBN 0 9535081 0 2

Front cover photograph: Joe Merrill (Bottom) and Amy Cockett (Titania) in *A Midsummer Night's Dream* – the Guild's first production in 1949
Photograph: Sport & General Press Agency

Back cover photograph: A scene from *Witness for the Prosecution* – the Guild's last production to date in 1990
Photograph: Edward Harris

Contents

Dedication		iv
Acknowledgements		iv
Author's note		v
Foreword		vi
Introduction		1
CHAPTER 1	*Beginnings*	3
CHAPTER 2	*The Story Unfolds*	13
CHAPTER 3	*End of a Tradition*	21
CHAPTER 4	*Local Drama Flourishes*	31
CHAPTER 5	*Mr Pepys Gets In on the Act*	43
CHAPTER 6	*Mixed Fortunes*	59
CHAPTER 7	*Time Moves On*	75
CHAPTER 8	*Taking Stock*	89
Index		101

Dedication

This book is dedicated to the group of people – some of them now dead – whose enthusiasm and hard work turned Bromley Theatre Guild from an idea into a reality.

Acknowledgements

Many people helped me in the creation of this book. My special thanks to Amy and Jack Cockett; Arthur Rochester; Vicky Pearce; Christine Howell (who suggested the idea in the first place) and Leigh Williams for its continuing support of theatre in the community.

Author's Note

When I was approached early in 1998 to write a history of Bromley Theatre Guild to celebrate its 50th anniversary I was delighted to be involved in a project that – coincidentally – had played a part in my life for many years.

My interest in, and love of, theatre was nurtured by my late father, Jim – an active member of *Beckenham Amateur Dramatic Society* – who called on me frequently in my formative years to 'hear his lines'. I should stress that I was a willing victim.

Later, when I pursued my career as a journalist, I was to become more closely involved with several local dramatic societies – and, indeed, the Guild itself. As Arts Reporter and subsequently Arts Editor of the *Kentish Times*, I reviewed many productions in the 70s and early 80s, carrying on a tradition that had been established by the likes of H.B.Hampton, Allan Holliday, Cliff Russell, Victor Thornton and David Shellan.

The printed word has the power to create as big a drama off stage as any you're likely to see on (Lord Willis did finally forgive me for the review I wrote of 'Mr Polly' at the Churchill Theatre in 1977) but hopefully there aren't too many Guild members who will look at the name of this author and shudder.

Researching the material for the book has been fascinating and there have been countless occasions in recent months when my absorption in old scrapbooks, letters, photographs and other Guild memorabilia has kept me at my small office in Beckenham long into the evening. Throughout, but particularly in the final weeks before deadline, my husband Ray has provided moral, as well as practical, support in helping to piece together the bits of the jigsaw.

The task has been demanding – and often daunting – but it's also been great fun and I shall remember it with affection.

Foreword

In this important world of theatre – for let's face it, at the end of a production all that is left are memories, anecdotes, a handful of photos and possibly a dodgy video – it is worth celebrating a 50th birthday.

For even though what we produce, what we create, is here today and gone tomorrow (and rightly so) it's proper that we celebrate longevities. As most of us know, good theatre doesn't happen overnight. It should only appear so.

Sir Alan Ayckbourn CBE

Introduction

The uninvolved probably think of the amateur theatre – or perhaps, in that redolent but outdated phrase, amateur 'dramatics' – simply as groups of people whose hobby is acting.

Certainly, the enjoyment of acting – and all the other essential activities which surround it – is fundamentally important. No theatre company is likely to be successful unless its members are enjoying themselves.

But the social implications go far beyond the pleasure of those taking part. Amateur theatre provides an essential cultural link, without which the community would be infinitely poorer.

At a time when regional theatres are fast disappearing and the West End prohibitively priced, many people's access to drama of any kind is solely through the medium of film or television. Yet no amount of digital electronic wizardry can replace the magic and the creativity of live theatre.

Here, each performance is a unique event, inviting performer and spectator to engage in a subtle interaction of artistic effort and audience appreciation – or not, as the case may be!

Creating successful live theatre is essentially a matter of teamwork. In this context the distinction between professional and amateur is irrelevant, except that the non-professional is more likely to be limited by time, money, space and materials. Success still comes only through the pooling of administrative, technical and artistic skills and through co-operation.

Each of Bromley's many theatre groups is, of course, a team, with its own peculiar strengths and limitations. Fifty years ago a number decided to join together in a larger team – a Theatre Guild, with the aim of encouraging mutual support and assistance and improving standards.

This book celebrates the first half century in pursuit of that aim. Regrettably, not all former member societies have survived and some current members have either been unable, or chosen not, to respond to the invitation to contribute. However, what follows does not set out to be a comprehensive history but rather a reflection of 50 years of progress through keen rivalry as well as shared endeavour.

Long may Bromley's amateur theatre flourish and continue to offer mental stimulation, companionship and, above all, enjoyment for all who care to seek it.

Arthur Rochester
Chairman, Bromley Theatre Guild

Chapter 1
Beginnings

Bromley Theatre Guild was born in the aftermath of the war years and the long, very depressing winter of 1947.

Soldiers were still coming home; rationing was in operation and young men continued to do their obligatory two years' National Service.

Drama groups – inevitably – were small and struggling, with materials for props, scenery and costumes hard to come by – and in some cases non-existent.

Ray of hope

A letter to the *Bromley & Kentish Times'* Amateur Stage column in September 1948 from Ken Ridley came as a ray of hope for a weary community. In it he suggested an idea for a confederation of dramatic societies in Bromley and the outlying district.

Letters of support followed, prompting the newspaper's popular editor and drama critic Allan Holliday to organise a conference in the old Public Library. With his customary zeal and good humour he managed to persuade delegates from 23 local drama groups to attend – with the result that *Bromley and District Amateur Theatre Guild* was created on February 13, 1949.

The aims of the newly created Guild were to:

1 Provide the largest possible degree of mutual support and assistance

2 Improve the general standard of production

3 Obtain as soon as practicable a central theatre for the specific use of member societies

A special logo was designed by Ian Allen – a student at Bromley College of Art

The Guild had 10 full member societies –

Bromley Players, *Bromley Home Guard Association Dramatic Society*, *Hayes Players*, *Merlin Players*, *The Quavers*, *The Radar Players*, *West Wickham Dramatic Society*, *Wickham Court Players*, *The Guildmore Players* and *St Luke's Amateur Dramatic Society*. Associate members were *Aperfield Players*, *Keston Amateur Dramatic Society*, *Holy Trinity Convent Dramatic Society* and *The Swift 10*.

Plans were soon under discussion for an adventurous open-air inaugural project – *A Midsummer Night's Dream* – to be staged in the grounds of Holy Trinity Convent in Plaistow Lane.

By June, local backers had agreed to provide the necessary funding and member societies got together to meet the professional director who would get *The Dream* off the ground – the 'charming and persuasive' Norman Gass.

(Such was the affection and respect he inspired that when he died, in Majorca, in September1989 many of the cast attended his funeral at Bellingham.)

Gass was an ex-Army colleague of the Guild's first chairman Gerald Williams and had an impressive reputation for staging Shakespeare in the open air.

The Dream was scheduled for September and willing hands offered help in every department to meet the challenge, among them Gerald's brother Maurice who planned the sets and the lighting.

Frank Maunder – a Guild stalwart who has also designed and built sets for *Hayes Players'* productions for many years – recalls how 'the old boys network' got things done for the Guild's debut.

Cable designated for a new council estate proved particularly useful; essential material for costumes found its way into the right hands; equipment for floodlighting was supplied by a local electrical company.

The common link was the *Bromley Home Guard Association* which had its own dramatic society.

An electrical and mechanical engineer by profession, Maunder 'fell into designing and building sets' and never looked back.

'I have played the odd walk-on part from time to time!', he says.

'I don't think there has been one cross word during the whole production and that is very unusual'.

Norman Gass speaking after the final performance of The Dream

Jack and Amy Cockett – who attended the Guild's inaugural meeting and who have played a diversity of roles on and off stage over the years – have fond memories of *The Dream*.

Newly-married and with a shared interest in amateur drama, they attended the first auditions, filled with enthusiasm at the prospect of playing

Forbes Robertson (Oberon), left; Jack Cockett (Puck) and Amy Cockett (Titania) in A Midsummer Night's Dream *presented by the Guild in 1949*
Photograph: Kentish Times

Shakespeare in an innovative floodlit production.

'We had no idea what our chances were but we were recalled for a second audition and within a week received a postcard notifying us that we had been cast as Puck and Titania', says Amy Cockett.

'We'd never considered the possibility of ending up as a couple of fairies and even checked that this was what the director actually meant. He did and there followed the most exciting few weeks of my life'.

'Jack Cockett was a superb Puck – a pocket-edition Lucifer on the one hand, he was the essence of life itself as the happy little sprite. I can find no fault here; his other-world postures and his speech left nothing to be desired'

G.R.C.T. writing in the Kentish Times

It was one of the hottest summers for nearly 20 years and the Cocketts, along with the rest of the company, slogged through a demanding schedule of rehearsals.

In addition to learning lines, Amy had also offered her services as a designer cum wardrobe hand and was given responsibility for Bottom's and the other rustics' costumes. She worked alongside two other designers and a team of volunteers who attended daily sewing sessions to supply costumes for the 32-strong cast.

Magical production

The production opened on September 7. Initially, the run was scheduled for six nights. It ran for eight and played to 4,000 people – a resounding success and a magical experience for everyone involved.

(Sadly, *The Dream*'s profits were swallowed up by having to reimburse the building firm for scaffolding – used to seat the audience – which was stolen from the site at the close of the show).

Says Amy of that first night: 'For all of us, starved of colour and excitement and sheer glamour, it was absolutely intoxicating – a warm evening, Mendelssohn's music, stars above real trees, a real moon.

'The Guild went on to do many more combined productions, a few of the early ones

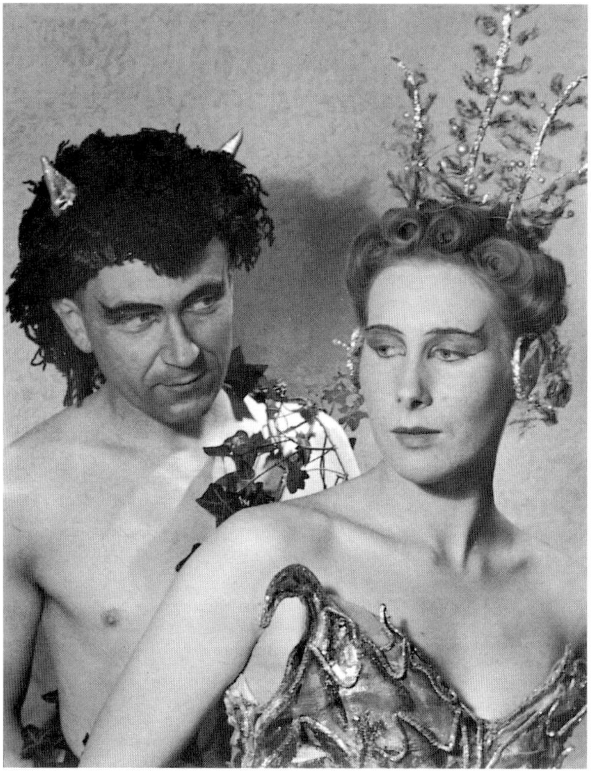

Jack Cockett as Puck and his wife Amy as Titania in The Dream
Photograph: D.G.Simmonds

Joe Merrill (Bottom) and Amy Cockett (Titania) in The Dream
Photograph: Sport & General Press Agency

again outdoors and with the same director, but the weather was never so kind again and they never reached quite such heights of achievement or inspired such enthusiasm, good will, commitment and friendship.

'Sometimes, in the attic, I come across the box which holds our costumes. There isn't much left of Jack's – just a leather cap with two miniature silver horns poking through a mass of green wool "hair". It still holds a faint evocative smell of spirit gum and greasepaint.

'I remember so clearly the agony he went through at rehearsals coping with the athletic interpretation of the character and how, in the early days of rehearsal, he was always too stiff in the morning to climb the bus stairs. Also, how his green body make-up repeatedly stained his clean underwear. I'd pray that no emergency would arise in which he was carted off to hospital!

'The silver lamé bodice of my dress is curling at the edges and the gauze skirt is torn and stained at the hem from walking in wet grass. Did I really have a waist as small as that? And did I really float through eight nights of sheer delight as Titania and fight with Oberon over my five year old 'changeling' boy?'

With rationing still in operation, costumes for *The Dream* demanded great ingenuity from the backstage team. Oberon and Puck wore men's long johns instead of tights (which were unobtainable) but by the time they were dyed and painted they were quite unrecognisable in their original form!

The *Bromley & Kentish Times* was unstinting in its praise of *The Dream*, no fewer than three members of staff reviewing the production.

Allan Holliday described Gass as 'plainly something more than a theatrical producer. He is an artist possessed of great ability and imagination', adding that it was doubtful if many who saw his interpretation would ever again be satisfied with a normal stage performance.

He praised the acting for its 'remarkably high level' and was clearly enchanted by the production's visual effects.

He wrote: 'It is well nigh impossible to give an impression of the loveliness of this production... As the tinted floodlights bathed the foliage in their soft radiance; as little pools of light came slowly into being in different parts of the glade, and as slowly faded from view; as the tall trees stretched upwards into the shadows with glimpses of the full moon between their boughs, the effect was almost intoxicating'.

Writing in the *Beckenham Journal* (later to be incorporated into the *Kentish Times*) its editor Victor Thornton (more of whom later) described it as an 'exquisite production... as a visual spectacle unrivalled in its beauty... with brilliantly designed and executed costumes contributing enormously to the pleasure'.

However, he took issue over the recorded music, maintaining that the production 'deserved much better'!

The Times Educational Supplement paid tribute to the 'excellent production's detailed grace and ingenious devices', saying it augured well for the future of the Guild.

And Robert Atkins – director of Regent's Park Open Air Theatre – complimented Gass on the 'amazing lighting', adding that Shakespeare would have given the company medals.

For Jack Cockett, 'Puck' paved the way for many theatrical credits (and awards) over the years but with a young family keeping her at home, Amy's future role with the Guild was to switch backstage.

Robert Atkins (left) congratulates producer Norman Gass
Photograph: Kentish Times

Costume Bureau launched

Following a production of Wilde's *The Importance of Being Earnest* at Bromley's New Theatre, for which Amy designed and made the costumes – she founded the Costume Bureau.

Under this immensely successful scheme costumes were hired to member societies at modest fees.

The Bureau was run from the Cocketts' home from 1961 until 1968 when it moved to Denmark Villas. It continued to flourish under Amy's supervision until December 1972 when she decided to return to business. That year Bromley Council announced that Denmark Villas was under threat of demolition.

Dorothy Runham stepped into Amy's shoes for a few months until Dora Coulson took charge. She remained for about three years, handing over the reins to Jane Janes who in turn passed it on to Margaret Cronk.

When the Guild staged Noel Coward's *Cavalcade* in 1972 Margaret was responsible for acquiring 200 costumes for the 46 actors. 'I was petrified!', she says.

After the move from Denmark Villas the Bureau had several homes, some more congenial than others!

'On one occasion the roof caved in and the clothes were absolutely soaked. When we moved to a scout hut it was even worse – no windows and no electric light.

'The best place was a scout hut at Bromley South where we remained until Waitrose was built in 1995'.

(In 1995 Guild costumes were leased to Yve Stone of *Theatre 62*, who set up her Green Room hire business with Guild support.)

Margaret enjoys making costumes – particularly for her favourite mid-Victorian period – and her handiwork has been seen on stage in numerous productions by her own society, *Hayes Players*.

Margaret's interest in the Guild was fostered by Stan Mole – an active chairman from 1979–1987 who has fought passionately over the years for the Guild's own premises. Despite the dream never becoming reality, he's not given up hope, even now!

Together with other committed Guild members – notably Joan Dutton – Stan worked tirelessly to make the annual fair and fête a success, watching assets rise from £1,000 to £8,000 in the 1980s.

A string of celebrity names were persuaded to 'open' these events (free of charge!) and in his resignation speech in March 1987 he paid tribute to David Jacobs, Lord Marsh, Frank Williams, Mary Peach, Roy Hudd and Lord Ted Willis.

Introduction of Festival Critics' Award

An example of Stan's determined streak is illustrated by the following incident!

One day he rang me at the *Kentish Times* and asked me my opinion on an idea he had for a 'Critics' Cup' at the Bromley Full Length Play Festival. I was dubious and said so.

'In theory it's a good idea but I'm not sure it's practical', I told him. 'Even with the (small) panel of critics at my disposal I can't guarantee we will see every production in the Festival and I don't think that would be fair'.

Stan persisted; I remained dubious – and the *Kentish Times* Critics' Award duly appeared!

Darryl McCarthy, who succeeded me as *Kentish Times* Arts Editor 12 years ago, has been closely involved in the selection of Critics' Award winners.

'Taking a critical stance means you are going to tread on a few feet here and there and, of course, there will be mistakes but I think the Guild has recognised the value of independent, informed criticism leading to a continuing, healthy relationship which is exemplified by the Critics' Award', he says.

In the past decade he has recorded the winding

up of several drama groups and seen many others struggle to recruit the new blood needed in order to sustain a worthwhile programme of performances.

'The challenge to find audiences today is much greater than it was in the wake of the last war when a sense of community was far stronger and alternative forms of entertainment were not available at the flick of a TV remote control or the click of a computer mouse'.

McCarthy acknowledges a steady rise in the overall quality of productions across the spectrum.

'From village halls to the redoubtable *Bromley Little*, the Guild embraces groups that refuse to mark time but regularly strike out to push further the boundaries of technical and acting achievement.

'The shows which break new ground may not draw the biggest audiences but drama has to be about the artistic fulfilment of those participating as well as the entertainment of their audiences'.

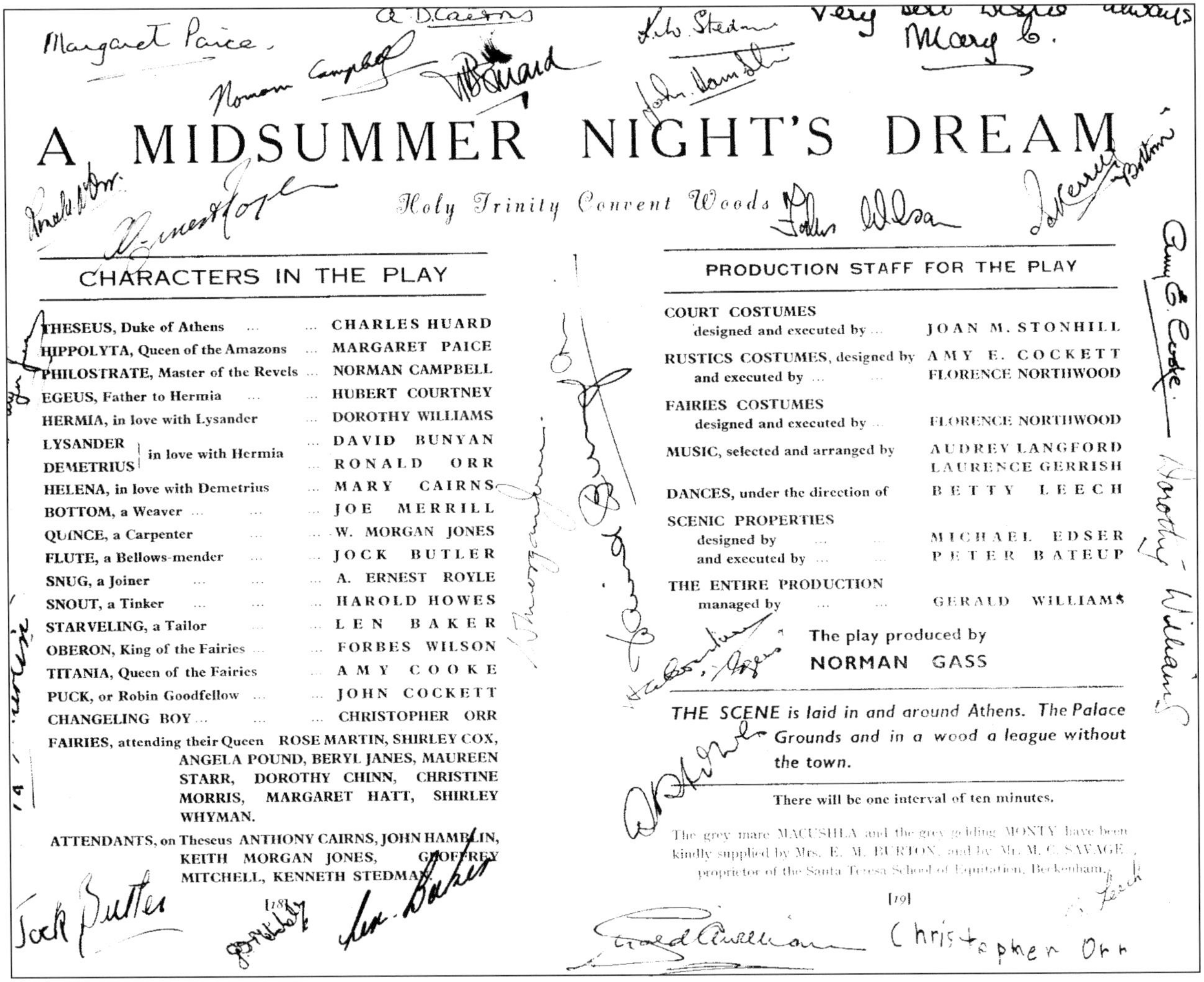

A MIDSUMMER NIGHT'S DREAM

Holy Trinity Convent Woods

CHARACTERS IN THE PLAY

THESEUS, Duke of Athens	CHARLES HUARD
HIPPOLYTA, Queen of the Amazons	MARGARET PAICE
PHILOSTRATE, Master of the Revels	NORMAN CAMPBELL
EGEUS, Father to Hermia	HUBERT COURTNEY
HERMIA, in love with Lysander	DOROTHY WILLIAMS
LYSANDER, in love with Hermia	DAVID BUNYAN
DEMETRIUS, in love with Hermia	RONALD ORR
HELENA, in love with Demetrius	MARY CAIRNS
BOTTOM, a Weaver	JOE MERRILL
QUINCE, a Carpenter	W. MORGAN JONES
FLUTE, a Bellows-mender	JOCK BUTLER
SNUG, a Joiner	A. ERNEST ROYLE
SNOUT, a Tinker	HAROLD HOWES
STARVELING, a Tailor	LEN BAKER
OBERON, King of the Fairies	FORBES WILSON
TITANIA, Queen of the Fairies	AMY COOKE
PUCK, or Robin Goodfellow	JOHN COCKETT
CHANGELING BOY	CHRISTOPHER ORR

FAIRIES, attending their Queen ROSE MARTIN, SHIRLEY COX, ANGELA POUND, BERYL JANES, MAUREEN STARR, DOROTHY CHINN, CHRISTINE MORRIS, MARGARET HATT, SHIRLEY WHYMAN.

ATTENDANTS, on Theseus ANTHONY CAIRNS, JOHN HAMBLIN, KEITH MORGAN JONES, GEOFFREY MITCHELL, KENNETH STEDMAN.

[18]

PRODUCTION STAFF FOR THE PLAY

COURT COSTUMES designed and executed by	JOAN M. STONHILL
RUSTICS COSTUMES, designed by	AMY E. COCKETT
and executed by	FLORENCE NORTHWOOD
FAIRIES COSTUMES designed and executed by	FLORENCE NORTHWOOD
MUSIC, selected and arranged by	AUDREY LANGFORD, LAURENCE GERRISH
DANCES, under the direction of	BETTY LEECH
SCENIC PROPERTIES designed by	MICHAEL EDSER
and executed by	PETER BATEUP
THE ENTIRE PRODUCTION managed by	GERALD WILLIAMS

The play produced by
NORMAN GASS

THE SCENE is laid in and around Athens. The Palace Grounds and in a wood a league without the town.

There will be one interval of ten minutes.

The grey mare MACUSHLA and the grey gelding MONTY have been kindly supplied by Mrs. E. M. BURTON, and by Mr. M. C. SAVAGE, proprietor of the Santa Teresa School of Equitation, Beckenham.

[19]

Signatures in the programme from members of A Midsummer Night's Dream *company*

Chapter 2
The Story Unfolds

The driving force behind the Guild's oldest member society – *Beckenham Amateur Dramatic Society* (the *BADS*) – was a professional actor – Martin Lewis.

A former producer (he worked at one time at the old Penge Empire), he appeared in the original West End production of Noel Coward's *Blithe Spirit* and was a member of the BBC Repertory Company.

Unlike many of his profession, he had a genuine love of amateur theatre which prompted him to found the *BADS* – known for the first three years of its existence as *The Raffaleans* – in 1923.

A perfectionist with a gift for drawing fine performances from players of little experience and, on occasions, only modest ability, he led the society for nearly 50 years.

When he died in 1970, the Rev Douglas Obee – himself a former *BADS* member – paid him this tribute at the funeral service in Beckenham Parish Church: 'We will remember him as a man of great personal charm and depth of character who understood and loved people for what they were'.

> 'The ladies of the cast receiving bouquets should only have one passed over the footlights. Any others to be placed on the stage from the wings'
>
> *BADS* Minute Book, 1925

Martin Lewis wasn't the only professional 'name' to be linked with the *BADS*.

At its inaugural production – *Raffles* – Dame Irene Vanbrugh, no less, gave a dramatic recitation between the acts.

Popular theatre and television actor Maurice Denham – for many years president of the society – says he owes his career to the *BADS*: a career that was launched, incidentally, in 1934 when he was asked to join Hull Repertory Company after being 'spotted' in a production of *Mary Rose* at the *BADS*' regular venue, Beckenham Public Hall.

(The Denham family were big supporters of the *BADS*, contributing in various ways behind the scenes).

The Scarlet Pimpernel *presented by the* BADS – *circa 1936*

Two other members in its early years – Kathleen Harrison and James Cossins – both went on to achieve real success in the profession.

(From time to time concerns have been expressed within the Guild as to whether members with professional connections should compete in the Bromley Festival. It is now generally agreed that they are free to do so, providing they have acted with the society they are representing for two years previous to the festival).

Even hardened newspaper men trod the boards at the Public Hall!

Victor Thornton – the respected editor (and theatre critic) of the *Beckenham Journal* (later incorporated into *Kentish Times Newspapers*) – 'drawled his way through a superb performance as Sir Percy Blakeney in *The Scarlet Pimpernel*', recalls a former *BADS* member.

Together with another *BADS* stalwart, Dorothy Carr, Thornton was a prime mover in the creation of Beckenham Children's Theatre which later evolved into *Beckenham Theatre Centre* with its own premises in Bromley Road.

Dorothy Carr acted as stage manager for the society on many occasions from the '30s onwards and was a professional writer of note, scripting pantomimes and plays that were produced nationally as well as locally.

Another successful venture of hers was to run the Beckenham Festival of Original One-Act Plays for many years.

Christine (left) and Sally Burgess in the BADS' *Music Hall in the 60s. Sally is now one of the UK's leading sopranos*

In the mid-60s – under the musical direction of the late John Hurst – the society launched into Old Time Music Hall. The 'side-line' proved immensely popular, enjoying a week's run at Bromley's *New Theatre* for many years in aid of Guild funds. Guest artists for the shows included Nicholas Parsons, Peter Glaze and Adelaide Hall.

Currently under the chairmanship of Michael Powell, now a professional actor who joined the *BADS* in the '60s, the society strives to maintain the early standards set by its peers.

Among the highlights of a varied repertoire are *Victoria Regina, Rose Without a Thorn, A Man for All Seasons, The School for Scandal, And So To Bed, The Boy Friend, Alice in Wonderland, An Ideal Husband, A Day in the Death of Joe Egg* and *The Barratts of Wimpole Street.*

Not having its own premises creates obvious headaches – particularly for the production team responsible for designing and building sets.

All the flats and equipment are stored in the basement of the Public Hall so Sunday mornings of a production week bring a combined assault from players and backstage team to lift everything needed from cellar to main hall!

Set builders and electricians then go to work with a vengeance to meet the Tuesday and Wednesday deadlines for technical and dress rehearsals.

Although the competitive spirit is keen – the society has had its share of success in the annual *Bromley Full Length Drama Festival* – it's not 'the be all and end all', says long-time member John Morris.

'Our aim is to have a strong season that is balanced with other activities for all our members'.

But to return to the fortunes of the Guild itself.

Rob Morris in The Norman Conquests, *presented by the* BADS *in 1997*

In October 1949 Colonel Norman offered the Guild a building site in Hayes Lane (next to the Baptist Chapel) for a small theatre but Kent County Council refused permission. The Guild lodged an appeal but by the following March when KCC reversed its decision the Guild's option on the site had lapsed.

Just before Christmas that year member societies organised the first dinner dance – at the Fantail in Farnborough (now Chapter One).

'Designer of the elaborate stage setting of *Pomander Walk* – young Michael Edser, former Beckenham Art School student – may never see the show. On National Service in the Forces, he is keeping in touch by 'remote control' and can only hope for leave...'

The Star – 4 August 1950

Pomander Walk

The Guild's second open-air production looked set to follow in the footsteps of *The Dream*.

Pomander Walk – a delightful period piece in the style of *Quality Street* – was staged in Church House Gardens (behind the Churchill Theatre), Bromley in September 1950.

Norman Gass again agreed to produce; 6,000 tickets were sold and the run was extended from seven nights to 10.

The elaborate, large-scale set – constructed on prefabricated lines like the ones used in film studios – depicted six Queen Anne style houses on the Thames Embankment at Chiswick.

It was a massive undertaking for the team of backstage workers (70 plus!) who battled against time to get it finished.

The youngest member of the cast was 21 year old Beryl Frisby who played the lovesick French girl Marjolaine.

Beryl will never forget the production. Just hours before the opening night, she developed a chest infection and a temperature of 100. She went to her doctor and insisted that she had to turn up for the performance as there was no understudy to replace her!

He gave her an injection of penicillin, drove her to Church House Gardens and sat in the front row during the performance in order to keep an eye on his patient.

Beryl made national headline news, telling a reporter of *The Evening News*:

'The doctor says I have bronchitis and will need three injections a day. He's doing his best to keep me going and believes I will be able to continue for the rest of the week'.

She did – but only because she followed his orders and stayed in bed each day until half an hour before the performance!

Beryl (her married name is Helder) recalls the production with the happiest of memories, saying she wouldn't have missed it for the world.

'I did feel ill and afterwards I had to stay in bed for the next six months to recover. I was off

Pomander Walk, *presented by the Guild – 1950*

sick for two years but I learned so much from Norman Gass – he was a wonderful director'.

Guy Verney (who was to become director of Bromley's *New Theatre*) was so impressed with Beryl's acting that he told her to keep in touch. Sadly, so much time passed that she was unable to pursue a professional acting career but her good friend Margaret Paice (a backbone of *St Luke's Amateur Dramatic Society*) suggested she went to *LAMDA* to train as a speech and drama tutor. She took her advice and never regretted it!

Cold weather may have kept some people away

but *Pomander Walk* received unanimous praise from the critics for its visual impact.

The *Bromley Mercury* described it as Bromley's 'most dazzling show', paying tribute to 'Miss Frisby's appealing beauty' while the *Beckenham Advertiser* wrote of the 'pure enchantment' of its stagecraft, adding that Gass had broken new ground.

Beryl Frisby in Pomander Walk.

In the *Beckenham Journal* Victor Thornton called the set 'extraordinarily successful' and the production 'visually delightful', citing Beryl Frisby 'a sensitive performer...and the most natural person in the arena'.

Allan Holliday in the *Bromley & Kentish Times* was equally admiring of both setting ('a resounding triumph for all concerned') and Beryl – 'she is completely captivating throughout and shows herself an astonishingly accomplished actress with a wide emotional range'.

Some of them were less happy with the play itself, however.

Victor Thornton again:

'*Pomander Walk* is a compound of sentimentality, archness and unsophisticated humour...a slow-moving play, the pace inevitably retarded on so broad and deep a stage'

And Allan Holliday:

'Even in a warm and comfortable theatre this production would have seemed overlong; in the cold air of a late September evening, on hard seats and with rugs around the knees, three acts lasting an hour each are just a bit much'.

These sentiments were obviously not shared by Robert Atkins (who surpassed himself on this occasion by declaring it the finest amateur show he had ever seen) or the audience, some of whom took the trouble to write to the local papers in its defence.

Chairman resigns

Nonetheless, the box office didn't cover the costs and this, together with the marked lack of volunteers to clear the production site, played a major part in the resignation of Gerald Williams as chairman.

As a result of an emergency meeting one of the Guild's financial backers – Ralph Allen – took his place.

About this time the roneo'd Guild newsletter, edited by Ken Ridley, evolved into a monthly printed publication and the editorship passed to Jack and Amy Cockett. (Less than two years later rising costs put an end to such refinements so it was back to roneo'd copies again!)

Early in 1951, plans for the Guild's Festival of Britain production (and its third open-air venture) – an adaptation of the Powell and Pressburger film *A Matter of Life and Death* – were abandoned due to the death of the producer Ronald Kerr, then director of Bromley's *New Theatre*.

The news was a tremendous shock to Guild members and the spring newsletter recorded his 'outstanding theatrical personality, great brilliance and charm'.

Kerr's successor was Guy Verney who agreed to produce the Guild's replacement show – Pinero's *The Gay Lord Quex* – at the *New*.

Among the cast was Joe Merrill – the Guild's first treasurer (and the founder of *Hayes Players*) who was a firm favourite with audiences after his performances in *The Dream* (Bottom) and *Pomander Walk* (Sir Peter Antrobus).

He shared the role of Sir Chichester Frayne with E.W.O'Clarey – a decision made by Verney who duplicated five of the principal characters so that more players would get the chance to appear.

Writing in the *Kentish Times*, H.B.Hampton pondered:

'The evening was a highly entertaining one...but the world has travelled far; morals, on the stage and off, have broadened and many of the moderns may find that the vices and virtues of nearly 70 years ago seem less serious than in these enlightened days...'

Unfortunately, the production coincided with a heatwave and box office returns were not as healthy as anticipated.

First One Act Play Festival

In the April of 1952 the Guild staged its first Drama Festival of One Act Plays at Stratford House School, Bickley.

Joe Merrill presented the Merrill Shield for Best Production and Robin Waldron the Waldron Shield for Best New Play.

Highlighted in the programme was the Guild's next open-air production – *Twelfth Night*.

Chapter 3
End of a Tradition

With *Twelfth Night* in 1952, the Guild returned to its traditional open-air setting – this time a woodland area between the junction of Madeira Avenue and Elstree Hill, Bromley.

Bromley College of Art designed the sets, the central feature of which was a staircase leading down from the hillside into a 'stage' skilfully fashioned from a small, disused quarry.

Norman Gass was back in the driving seat and hand picked a strong cast from 14 member societies for another of his innovative offerings. The only guest actor was Stuart Ready who played Malvolio. A professional playwright, his sketch at the Palladium called *I Want to be an Actor* starred Mary Pickford, Chesney Allen and Tommy Trinder.

Artistically, the production was a triumph. I can't find any quibbles among the critics, all of whom eulogised Gass' interpretation ('stupendous piece of work'; 'pageant of rare beauty'); the cast and the visual effects.

Music for the production was selected and arranged by Audrey Langford and the songs were sung by Philip Winter (later to play Samuel Pepys in the Guild's production of *And So To Bed*) who received a special mention from the unnamed *Kentish Times* reviewer for his fine rendering. Philip's wife Joan (later Mrs Pepys) was also in the cast.

Financially, however, *Twelfth Night* was a disaster and finally put paid to the Guild's open-air enterprises.

Despite the urgings from the newspapers not to miss the production, appalling weather kept many potential audiences firmly at home, with the result that a mere 3,000 attended the 11-night run. The crisis was deepened by a debt of nearly £300 to the backers of *Pomander Walk*.

The Guild's annual meeting in the February of 1953 was something of a watershed. Chairman Councillor Ralph Allen told members there was no chance of future open-air productions unless they found a way to offset the losses. Meanwhile, they had to 'lick their wounds and get strong again'.

Secretary Robin Waldron was more forceful. 'If you want the Guild you must work for the Guild. You cannot expect it all to be done for you by a few willing people'.

These sentiments were to be echoed over the

A scene from the Guild's production of Twelfth Night *in 1952*

years by other Guild officers but at the time they sent shock waves through its members, particularly when Waldron proposed, at the next annual meeting in February 1954, that the Guild be dissolved because 'it had outlived its usefulness and was in danger of dying from apathy and declining membership'.

The troops rallied, claiming they had been brought to their senses, and the motion was defeated by 36 votes to seven. Several spoke against the proposal. Margaret Paice suggested a firm gesture should be made to the guarantors that Guild shows and other functions would aid funds; Amy Cockett (by now a member of *St*

Luke's and a staunch believer in a Guild future) felt it had a moral obligation to continue and Ruth Cooper advised smaller productions as an option.

(Light relief at this crucial meeting was provided by Harold Armstrong who quoted an epitaph to a baby: '*Since I was so quickly done for, I wonder what I was begun for*'.)

In the spring of that year the third One Act Drama Festival – at St Luke's Church hall – attracted nine entries. The newly-formed *Green Room Club* won the Merrill Shield for the greatest all-round excellence for the second year running and Margaret Paice won the Waldron Shield for the best original play – *Exile from England* performed by *St Luke's ADS*.

Margaret's links with *St Luke's* were forged after she produced a one-act play for a Parish 'social' in October 1947. The vicar was so impressed with her efforts that he invited her to form a drama group.

Long association

It was the start of a long and devoted association to the society, for whom she produced 30 plays and won a special Guild Adjudicator's Award for services to local drama.

A *LAMDA* gold medallist and elocution teacher, her first production was *Candied Peel* in 1948 and her last – Coward's *This Happy Breed* – was in 1985. Sadly, she died in July 1998 – six years after the closure of the society – but she was an honoured 'guest' at a reunion in 1997 marking the 50th anniversary of *St Luke's* inception.

All the church's vicars in its lifetime – Canon Hasard-Short and the Revs Appleton, Osborn and Smith – were great supporters of the society which quickly took on a personality and became a prominent member of the Guild.

In the early days it presented two productions a year – in the spring and the autumn – but in 1951/2 it progressed to three plays a season, encouraging new producers into the fold. Among them was Bill Walker who brought melodrama back to Bromley with his production of *Dirty Work at the Crossroads*. (So impressed was Allan Holliday that he returned for a second performance and the interest sparked off a local revival including one at the *New*!).

Among other major producers were Jack Cockett (who joined the society with his wife Amy in 1951), Peter Rodway, Ken Bannister, Vera Hughes, Stan Ward and Cyril and Joy James.

The varied seasons sometimes included original revues and pantomimes; Music Hall and, in 1961, a spoof western called *The Legend of Luke Saint* – written and composed by Rodway with members of *Glebe Knoll Players* playing the baddies!

Over 45 years the society presented 97 full-length plays, 22 one-act plays and 21 Christmas Evenings – the latter devised by Rodway's actress sister, Sonia. This much-loved tradition began in 1969 when the church decided to replace equipment in the hall (*St Luke's* 'home'). Sonia suggested a concert of Christmas words and music with a retiring collection donated to the hall fund and, with committee approval, duly organised a programme of carols, poetry and prose readings with hot punch and mince pies prepared and served by members in costume. (Sonia stage-managed 17 of these evenings including the last in 1990).

The society was a keen competitor in the Bromley Festival, achieving some notable awards in its time, but despite winning the Runner Up Best Production category twice (for *The Family Reunion* produced by Vera Hughes in 1974 and *Playbill* produced by Peter Rodway in 1977) it never took the top prize.

Flying the flag at the Guild's combined shows along with Margaret Paice and the Cocketts were David Weller, Ruth Spon, Bill Walker, Peter and

A scene from The Legend of Luke Saint, *presented by* St Luke's ADS *in 1961*

Sonia Rodway and Vera, Michael and Christina Hughes.

St Luke's had its own newsletter, launched under the editorship of Paul Beauchamp in 1976. Subsequent editors were Fred Humble, Richard Weller, Peter Rodway, David Weller, Graham Bate and Jack and Amy Cockett.

In 1958 *St Luke's* presented the trophy for Best Set in the Bromley Festival in memory of Sylvia Love – a gifted scenic artist who was an active performer as well as a set designer. The trophy was designed and produced by a Farnborough craftsman.

In the final edition Cockett, then chairman of the society, had this to say: 'Shakespeare wrote "...a good play needs no epilogue". Can the same be said of *S.L.A.D.S.* – a good dramatic society which has given a great variety of entertainment to the community, which has forged many friendships, weathered many storms and established a fine reputation!...The curtain is now down but it was a good play. No epilogue!'

(One tragic note is recorded in the society's history that I feel I should include here. In the early '50s one of its popular members – Lilian Burton – moved to Rhodesia – now Zambia – with her husband and family. Four years later she was attacked by an African mob and died some days later).

Although *Beckenham Amateur Dramatic Society* can claim to be the oldest of the Guild's members, three other societies were launched a few years later in the early '30s – *Bromley Little Theatre, Hayes Players* and *Chelsfield Players.*

Bromley Little Theatre (*BLT* or *The Little* as it is also known) began life as the *Bromley Little Theatre Movement* – the creation of its 24 year old founder H. Wilson Pook.

With a membership of just 14, its inaugural production *And So To Bed* was staged at the Bromley Country Club in Crown Lane.

But Pook had ambitions for his own theatre and in 1936 an opportunity presented itself in the shape of the derelict and vacant ex-Co-op bakery in North Street. He acquired the lease, designed the conversion and watched his dream become a reality.

'I ran *Bromley Little* as a sort of benevolent dictatorship but I was always open to suggestions', he says. 'In the event we all got on very well. I fought for as high a standard as could be expected from amateurs for only in this way could we hope to build and maintain a loyal audience necessary for our survival'.

In 1938 Pook had to relinquish *BLT* to pursue his scientific and commercial ventures, 'handing it over' to Colonel John Leather and his actress wife Betty Pinchard.

For 60 years *BLT* has presented a play each month (except for August when it undergoes necessary refurbishment) – no mean feat considering it has never received a grant or

A scene from A Christmas Carol, *presented by* St Luke's ADS *in 1971*

subsidy and is completely independent financially. A private theatre club, it is run by and for its members who pay a modest annual subscription.

The Little's president is the actor Michael York whose links with the club were forged in the late 50s as a pupil at Bromley Grammar School. He was asked by his English teacher, Grace Collett-Franklin – a 'pillar' of *BLT* – to take part in her production there of *My Three Angels*.

York writes in his autobiography: 'I responded immediately and positively – not only because she was offering one of the leading convict roles. This studio theatre and its semi-professional company had a considerable reputation and was run by an extraordinary old lady (Betty Pinchard) who was as dynamic as she was opinionated'.

The '*Little*'s' ghost

York also makes reference to the *BLT* ghost.

'One night after rehearsals the silence was eerily interrupted by shuffling, muffled footsteps and we [York's fellow actor, Adrian Brine] both felt a sudden and distinct chill in the air. Perhaps it was just tiredness but it certainly "froze our young blood and made each particular hair to stand on end" in vivid confirmation of Hamlet Senior's experience'.

Since its inception, *BLT*'s aim has been to present exciting theatre at a reasonable cost.

Bill Morley – a member since the mid-60s, during which time he has directed numerous productions and held various offices (he's currently Publicity Co-ordinator) – recalls his first audition with Betty Pinchard.

'She was certainly a very formidable lady. Apparently, she once sent a note round to Lawrence Olivier saying she couldn't hear and he sent her an apology!'

Morley says that *BLT* is constantly 'pushing the boundaries' of its repertoire in order to get away from the comedy/thriller pattern. In planning its season of plays it tries to ensure all tastes are met but its over-riding goal is quality. To this end it has created an artistic team of five members, one of whom is assigned to each production to act as a 'helping hand'. At the end of the run the team meets up for a post mortem.

Unlike the early days when members (Morley included) had to sign a contract preventing their involvement with another company, there are no restrictions on *BLT* actors who often 'float' between a network of local theatres such as *Bob Hope*, *Edward Alderton* and *Geoffrey Whitworth*.

One need look no further than the 1999 season to get a flavour of the *Little*'s diversity. A World Premiere – *Doctor Y*; Harold Pinter's *Old Times*; Shakespeare's *Twelfth Night* and David Hare's *Skylight* are among the planned productions.

The 1995 production of Our Country's Good *won* BLT *five awards in the Bromley Festival of that year including Best Production and Best Producer (Bill Morley)*

The Crucible *presented by* BLT – *1961*

The Crucible *presented by* BLT – *1996*

Chapter 4
Local Drama Flourishes

A conversation between two commuters travelling from Hayes to Charing Cross was to lead to the formation of *Hayes Players*. The commuters were Joe Merrill and Doreen Barry (who subsequently acted with *Hayes Players* before marrying a fellow Player – Jack Soper – and emigrating to Australia).

Both Merrill and Doreen were convinced of the need for a drama group in the community and recruited some new members, among them Frank Marjoriebanks and Sullivan Mortimer – the organist at Hayes Parish Church.

The first production – *Undercurrents* – in March 1934 was written by a friend of Merrill's, Claud Holt. The venture generated so much enthusiasm that Emlyn Williams' *A Murder Has Been Arranged* followed in May.

Sixty years on and still going strong! Winnie Pellow – currently a Vice President of *Hayes Players* – appeared in the 1935 production of *The Sport of Kings*

With an impressive output of three or four plays each season, the society entered the *News Chronicle All England Drama Festival* in 1937 with Priestley's *Mystery at Greenfingers*. It finished a creditable 18th out of 200 entries and second in the south of England area finals.

Although its wartime productions were spasmodic, it staged plays for *Bromley Home Guard Association* taking *The Man Who Stayed at Home* to 16 different camps, including RAF Biggin Hill.

Cramped cellar

For many years members rehearsed and built sets in a cramped cellar beneath a dress shop (*Vanda's* or *Marjorie's*) in Station Approach. In the late '60s they rented 'luxury accommodation' in George Lane – a large outhouse – until it was redeveloped in the early '70s.

Luckily, members were then able to rent a vacant plot of land on Hayes Farm and they built their own rehearsal space/workshop and storage area which they named *The Merrill Studio* in memory of their founder.

Says Ron Whytock: 'Amateur drama in Hayes and the Hayes Players in particular owe a deep debt of gratitude to Joe Merrill who was not only a leading actor with the company but also a director'.

The studio was built entirely by members under the direction of Reg Purcell and Derek Moore and there are those who still recall the arrival of a lorryload of ready-mixed cement and the willing, but inexperienced, volunteers who laboured to get it properly laid before it set!

After 25 years, the studio is coming to the end of its useful life and a special fund has been launched to raise cash for a new building. It is hoped that there will be additional Lottery funding.

It's interesting to note that the *Hayes Players'* base was never far from a pub – initially *The New Inn* and subsequently *The George*!

A scene from Precious Bane, *presented by* Hayes Players *in 1986*

Although the society aims to strike a balance in its productions, incorporating 'challenging plays' into its repertoire, it is acutely aware of its audience's likes and dislikes and positively encourages input. It mounts four productions annually, always making a profit, and sells between 70% and 80% of its available tickets.

February and April productions are entered in the Bromley and Kent Festivals where it has achieved considerable success, winning Kent on five occasions and Bromley on 13.

Hayes Players has close connections with other groups in the community – notably Hayes Village Association and Hayes Horticultural Society –

A scene from Men Should Weep, *presented by* Hayes Players *in 1987*

and has always been a keen supporter of Guild activities, members having been involved in many of the combined shows from the early days to the final one: *Witness for the Prosecution*. (Steve Williams and Kathy and Ted Silk all participated in this venture at the *Churchill Theatre*).

Ron Mackay was Guild secretary for 13 years (a Ron Mackay Cup is awarded annually at Bromley Festival for Best Actor in a Minor Role); Kathy Silk was also a Guild secretary; former *Hayes Player* Steve Williams was chairman and is now development officer; Alex Clark is its current treasurer and Graham Finch its president.

Finch – who has also held three other Guild posts (and has won the Best Actor award at three Bromley Festivals) – still cherishes the hope that the 'combined show' (abandoned in 1990) will be revived, though he is aware of the problems.

'Member societies are involved in their own productions leading up to April and October which leaves the summer and that's the least attractive time because of holidays', he says.

'I would like to see combined shows for a period of say three years and then have a break for a year or two'.

Chelsfield takes off

Around the time the idea for the *Hayes Players* was being discussed on a train, young couples settling into the Chelsfield Park Estate decided to get together to read and perform plays.

One member of the group – Mabel Fredericks – had an extension built onto her house which was designed as a mini-auditorium seating 50. The audience sat on raised benches.

The first production was *20th Century Lullaby* and the role of the Madonna was played by Ellen

The Brontes, *presented by* The Chelsfield Players *in 1988*

Blatcher – the mother-in-law of the society's current chairman Ann Blatcher.

As membership grew, so did the need for larger premises which included St Mary's Church Hall in Green St Green and the Civic Hall in Orpington. Finally, urged on by a dream to perform in their own village hall in Chelsfield, the company teamed up with other local groups to raise funds and the dream became a reality. The society took the name *Chelsfield Village Hall Dramatic Society*,

Blithe Spirit, *presented by* The Chelsfield Players *in 1992*

changing it in 1949 to *The Chelsfield Players*.

Despite being small in numbers, the society has a reputation for its varied repertoire and boasts two prominent names in the entertainment business among its past membership: the radio DJ Brian Matthew and actor David Jason.

'Brian Matthew was a very active member of the society and it was he who introduced David and his brother (Arthur White)', says Ann Blatcher. 'But there are no "stars" in *The Chelsfield Players*. Being such a small group it is essential that everyone helps in all aspects of putting on a play. The lead in one production can find themselves in charge of props for the next or with a small walk-on part. I started off selling programmes in 1962!'

Two full length plays are produced annually plus a short play in the summer – at one time in members' gardens but latterly in public grounds.

Four society launches in the '40s

In addition to *St Luke's ADS* (highlighted in the previous chapter) the '40s brought four new launches prior to the Guild's debut at the end of the decade – *Farnborough Dramatic Society* in 1943; *Orpington Amateur Repertory Club* and *West Wickham Pantomime Society* in 1945 and *Bromley Players* in 1946.

For the first two years of its life, *Farnborough Dramatic Society* was, in fact, a drama class presenting one-act plays and entertainment evenings under the critical eye of its inspired founder – Dorothy St Clare Shadwell, a speech and drama teacher for the Kent Education Committee.

By 1943 the company had the confidence to stage its first full-length play – *The Ghost Train* – but it wasn't until the '50s that it adopted its proper name, since when it has staged three plays a year at Farnborough Village Hall.

Audience participation

Being a village society, it is fortunate in having a regular supportive audience who in the past would think nothing of returning the odd stray prop which had fallen off the stage or participating in other ways.

During a performance of the thriller *Wait Until Dark* in 1969 the scene was set for the villain of the piece to set fire to the blind heroine's flat. However, in the preceding action the actress had flung a vase of water with such abandon that both the villain and his matches were drenched.

In the deafening silence that followed an ever-helpful Thursday night regular stepped into the breach by offering his own matches with the comment: "Want a light mate?"

The society joined the Guild in 1972, taking part in many of the combined shows (most notably *Tom Jones*, for which it supplied actors, builders, box office and bar management) and competing in the Bromley Festivals.

It won three acting awards for its first Festival entry – *Blithe Spirit* – but 1972 was the year of

FDS *in its first pantomime* Cinderella *in 1978*

the power cuts and the night the adjudicator attended the production the company held its breath in anticipation of the inevitable blackout.

Luckily, it didn't happen but car headlamps and 'borrowed' dustcart batteries were on hand to keep the stage illuminated just in case!

The society's chairman Edna Walker (a seasoned Festival winner) says that adjudications have been invaluable to *FDS* over the years – encouraging the society to seek ever higher standards – but the biggest boost to morale came in 1982 when it landed the award for Runner Up

The 1993 50th anniversary production The Militants *involving every member of* FDS

Best Production with *Shop at Sly Corner*.

In 1978 the society ventured into pantomime with *Cinderella*, following up with *Dick Whittington* and *Aladdin* with decent intervals in between. Since the writer moved to France (could there be a connection?) any suggestion of the word is greeted with looks of horror.

Occasionally, productions are staged in other venues. One such project – *Isolation at Eyam* – at St Giles the Abbot Church evokes particular memories.

Says Edna Walker: 'This one act play gives an account of the 1665 Plague and its effects on a Derbyshire village which is closed by the local Reverend to stop the spread of the disease. The exact timing of the curfew was to be signalled by the ringing of the church bell. St Giles' bell was very heavy and the backstage ringer's legs very short so it was only a matter of divine providence that the tension of the climax wasn't shattered by the aerial flight of a wayward campanologist!'

Pet actors

Two pet dogs have earned mentions for their endeavours. Pepi was the first to make his acting debut with *FDS* but not only did he get stage fright and was sick in the wings but also made an unscheduled appearance after he had supposedly died!

The second – Snuffy – fared better. A most accomplished actor, he played the role of Helen Keller's dog in *The Miracle Worker* in 1991, leaving the stage unescorted at each performance. (What the audience didn't see, however, were the biscuits waiting for him in the wings!)

In 1997 the company joined in the centenary celebrations of the Village Hall providing a popular repertoire of songs, monologues and once-act plays throughout the proceedings, while at the same time serving tea and cakes dressed as Lyons Corner House 'Nippies' – and that was just the chaps!

FDS has been winning Bromley Festival awards in numerous categories since 1972.

Vi Simper is the society's longest serving member with an unbroken record of 39 years. In 1989 – when she was in her 70s – she won Best Costumes' award in the Festival for *A Letter from the General* for which she made more than 30 costumes

'Interested thespians'

In the summer of 1945 an advert appeared in the local press asking for interested thespians to attend an inaugural meeting at Holy Trinity Parish Church.

Fourteen people responded, among them Founder President Dorothy Hall, and the *Orpington Amateur Dramatic Society* was born.

Local traders proved very supportive of the new drama group. Tickets were sold from a shop in the High Street; Greaves furniture store regularly supplied a variety of items; a log fire appeared constantly, courtesy of the London Electricity Board and Bretts, the ladies' milliner, produced hats for all the productions.

In the early days the society donated a large percentage of its profits to local organisations – particularly the church which was urgently in need of funds to restore the church hall. As a 'thankyou' the boy scouts agreed to deliver handbills – a noble gesture as at times there were as many as 4,000!

As television became an increasingly competitive leisure activity, profits began to dwindle so the group was forced to rely on jumble sales to boost its cash flow.

Unenviable task

Publicising shows is always an unenviable task but an incident during a production of *The Brides of March* brought the group to the attention of a much wider audience than the local community.

The 1985 production of A Woman of No Importance, *presented by* OARC

While the actresses were on stage for the 'harem' scene their handbags were stolen from the dressing room.

The *Evening News* reported the theft under the headline *Harem Girls Lose All* which doubtless boosted the Box Office at the following evening's performance!

Les Townley proved a tower of strength as a publicity organiser. Among the stunts he engineered were getting the female members of *Outside Edge* to appear in bikinis outside Chelsfield Village Cricket Pavilion one February and taking a pantomime cow to Safeway to advertise *Jack and the Beanstalk*.

The society's junior section (sadly, disbanded in 1991 after more than 21 years) was the first of its kind in Orpington.

Its aim was to provide speech and drama training to youngsters between 12 and 18 but because the numbers had to be limited to 25 students each year the waiting list was never ending.

The annual fee was 75p, rising ultimately to £1, and the self-financing group raised money through jumble sales, craft fairs, coffee mornings and boutiques.

All profits went to charities of the students' choice and over the years hundreds of pounds were raised for a wide variety of good causes.

Every other year students staged a show at the Civic Hall (now called the Crofton Hall and the society's regular venue since 1949) followed by a drama workshop in alternate years. The shows, written specially for the group to avoid royalties, proved immensely popular – due, in no small part, to the efforts of John and Ruth White; Roger Sammons; Derek Cadde, Vera and Ted Lane and a staunch backstage team.

Merger

When the society merged with the Proscenium Club in the mid-50s it changed its name to *Orpington Repertory Club*, adding the 'amateur' in 1968. Diane Parslow recalls the numerous changes in rehearsal venues – some more comfortable than others!

'Memories spring to mind of rehearsals in a scout hut throughout a freezing cold winter with dripping tents often hanging from the rafters and the restaurant above the Commodore Cinema where trays of fatty cold potatoes stood in readiness for the next day's lunch', she says.

Surprisingly, it wasn't until 1984 that *OARC* staged its first pantomime: now an important part of the repertoire every two years with a loyal following of cubs, brownies, guides and scouts.

The company has learned a lot since its first panto, *Cinderella*, when children were invited up on stage to sing to Daisy the Cow who was 'unable' to moo. There was a stampede and the apron stage began to creak under the strain.

Nowadays, the director is more circumspect about numbers!

A lottery bid in the spring of 1998 failed but the society intends to try again, meanwhile pursuing its diverse fund-raising activities to ensure its survival.

OARC has won many Bromley Festival awards including five for *Daisy Pulls It Off* in 1992.

The 1992 production of Daisy Pulls It Off *which won five awards for* OARC *in the Bromley Festival including Best Production*

CHAPTER 5
Mr Pepys Gets In on the Act

West Wickham Pantomime Society has its roots in the *Home Guard* which decided to stage a pantomime in 1945 in aid of local children's societies. When it was disbanded the annual panto had become something of a tradition so rather than let it die, *WWPS* was specially created to carry on the good work.

A few years ago when it celebrated its 50th anniversary one of its celebrity Patrons, Simon Oates, attended the special Gala Night while others – Roy Hudd, Tony Hatch, Jackie Trent, Pat Coombs and Sally Burgess – all sent their good wishes.

Roy Hudd was actually moved to write a special poem for the occasion:

The flag you've all kept flying
So congratters are now due,
Through thick and thin each Christmas
You've produced brand new
Crusoes and Aladdins,
Puss in Boots and Mother Goose,
You've done 'em all and this year
Cinderella'll be let loose.
Half a century of fun;
Your shows? No-one can lick 'em,
Panto's surely in good hands
With the Guys and Gals of West Wickham.

The Gala Night raised £560, to which the society added £575 of donation funds which went to the physiotherapy unit at Bromley's Phoenix Resources Centre.

Pat Coombs, who was an active *WWPS* member in her youth, is very supportive and recently sent the society the original of a *Babes in the Wood* script written by her mother.

Over the years the society has made countless and varied donations to local charities. Among the many to benefit from its generosity are a young victim of cerebral palsy who received his own lap top computer; pupils with learning difficulties at Dartford's Milestone School who now enjoy percussion instruments and a blind person who has his own guide dog.

Since it was founded the society's permanent home has been Wickham Halls. So close has the association been, in fact, that when the halls were facing financial ruin members mounted a rescue package to keep them functioning.

Says Amanda Pooley: 'Members now work actively as trustees resulting in continuing improvement to the facilities for the society and other hall-users alike. Hi-tech equipment, including a new lighting and sound board, means we can stage a really professional show and we are currently seeking permission to instal a lighting tower.

'Our stock of costumes is ever increasing as are our props and the new Clavinova (electric piano) brings a wonder of sounds to the performances!'

WWPS's *1995 version of* Cinderella

The society's repertoire also includes summer shows which take the form of Old Time Music Halls, 'end of pier' and variety shows. (Recently it scored a considerable hit with *Musical Memoirs* – devised and acted by *WWPS* members and featuring numbers from some of the best loved musicals such as *South Pacific*, *Cabaret* and *Oliver!*).

The society has its own costume department which boasts more than 1,000 items to ensure the casts uphold their strong reputation!

Best track record? Linda Shepherd joined *WWPS* as a dancer in 1962 and hasn't missed a panto since!

WWPS's *Music Hall in 1993*

Students plea for drama class

A group of young students at Bromley and West Wickham Evening Institute were instrumental in launching the *Bromley Players*. In 1946, keen to see a drama class included in the syllabus, they had approached the principal with the idea.

Marjorie Herbert joined the institute (run under the adult education scheme) as tutor and founded the society which staged four productions a year – mainly in the hall of Bromley

Cranbrook, *presented by the* Bromley Players *– 1954*
Photograph: Studio Cole

Boys Grammar School in Hayes Lane. Rehearsals were held on the first floor of the brick building in the corner of the grounds which later became an ambulance station.

Other early venues were Bromley Parish Church hall – later demolished – and Farnborough Hospital.

Marjorie Herbert produced and cast all the plays, some of the members joining via her other evening class in stagecraft, voice production and public speaking.

In 1950 the institute moved to Springhill – a large old house on the site of the present roundabout at the junction of London Lane and College Road – which proved an ideal rehearsal and storage space. Productions were staged in St Augustine's Church hall and later in the Robert Whyte Memorial Hall in London Lane.

Marjorie left the group in 1952 (her swansong was *Great Day*) to be succeeded as tutor by Hilda Trowbridge, Barbara Hood and subsequently George Burnett.

Rosemary Harris (who joined the group in 1953 and was tutor from 1960–71, producing more than 30 shows along the way), says that constant changes of performance venue created quite a few headaches for the cast.

'I have memories of climbing in and out of windows at one church hall in order to enter from the other side of the stage. One night a poorly sighted actor got lost on the way round and failed to make his entrance!

'Sometimes we found ourselves without a hall at the last minute and for *Skin of our Teeth* the hall had been double booked. We managed to get Wickham Hall but had to cut the scenery down to size. The dress rehearsal finished just before curtain up!'

The *Bromley & Kentish Times* duly recorded the incident, its reviewer Cliff Russell commenting: 'It was a triumph over adversity, epitomising the fine spirit of drama enthusiasts locally'.

Bromley Players suffered more than its fair share of problems over performance venues as the *Bromley & Kentish Times* repeatedly highlighted:

'The society is in trouble again. After losing a chance of obtaining new members at the beginning of the season because of an adult education administrative slip-up, it is now trying to find another hall following a belated veto on the use of Bromley Technical College'

Because it was an evening institute, class membership varied considerably and the majority of students were eager to put their newly acquired skills to the test as soon as possible. Large cast plays were essential, says Rosemary.

Finances were always tight (subscriptions went to the Council) so jumble sales were a necessary form of survival but the group often gave charity

Kathy Silk and Ray Harris in The Pillars of Society, *presented by the* Bromley Players *in the 60s*

performances, carrying on a tradition of its early years.

Many of the *Players* – among them Rene Hughes, Bob Miles, Kathy and Ted Silk, Ray Harris (Rosemary's husband), Marjorie Waldron, Pauline Broad, Paul and Juliet Davis, Ian James, Paul Butler and Patricia Hammond (who later formed the Patricia Hammond Theatre School) – gained valuable experience in acting, producing and backstage before joining other societies.

Looking at the list of credits (*The Crucible*, *Sweeney Todd*, *A Christmas Carol*, *Candida* for example) there appears to have been no hesitation in facing a challenge but despite its resourcefulness, the society struggled in its final years.

After Rosemary resigned in 1971 a replacement tutor was never found. In the last four years of its existence, the society was run as a club with members Irene Whitehead and Rene Hughes acting as guest producers. A new Theatre Backstage workshop was launched on Friday evenings with the *Players*' stage manager – the late John Townsend – as tutor.

Pauline Broad and Ray Harris in Sweeney Todd, *presented by the* Bromley Players *in the 60s*

Guild makes a 'comeback' with Pepys

In 1955, with a fourth One Act Play Festival under its belt (organised for the second year running by Jack Cockett), the Guild made plans for its fifth combined show.

It had been three years since the debate over its future but with an indoor venue – the *New* – and the assistance of the theatre's scenic designer

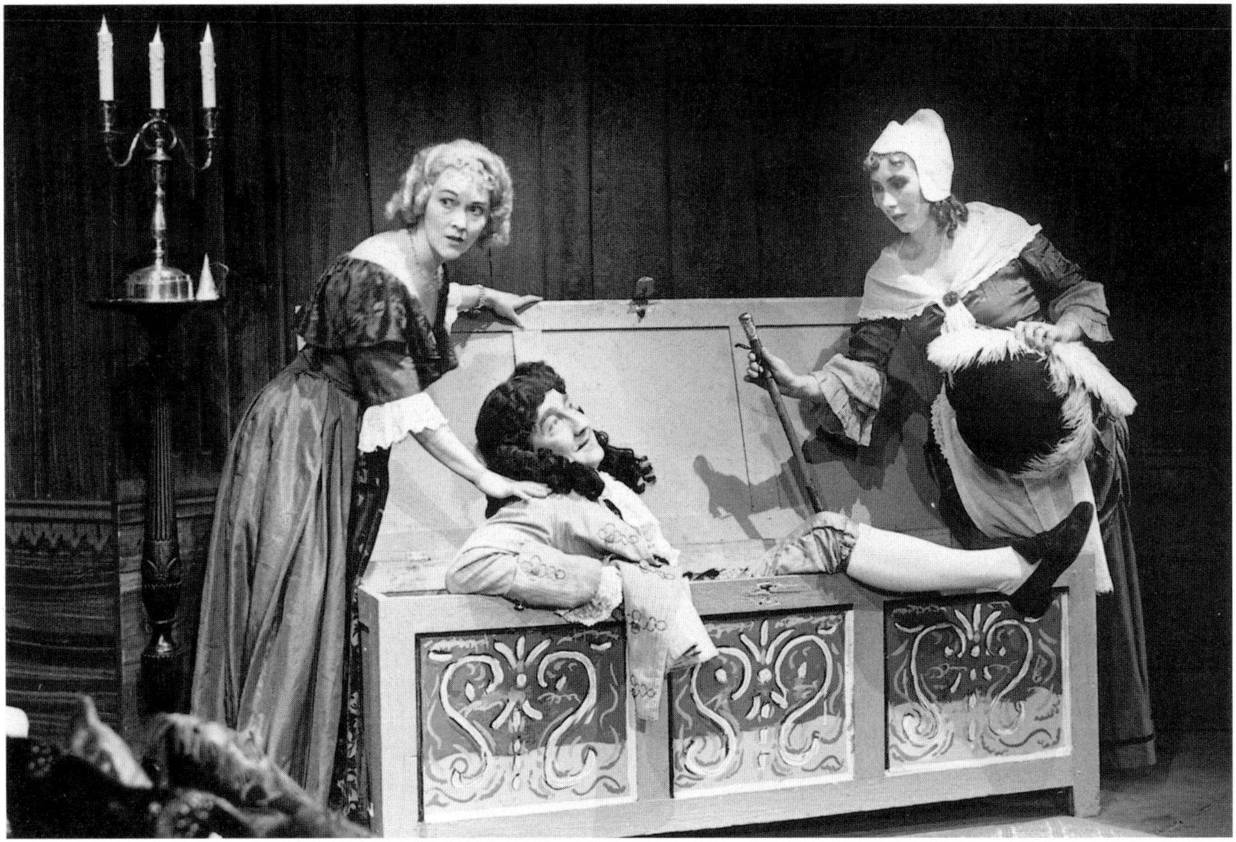

Philip Winter as Pepys with (left) Patrica Lee and Amy Cockett in the Guild's production of And So To Bed *in 1955*
Photograph: Photo Functions

Henry Graveney, producer Elsie Lindsey was off to a flying start with the restoration comedy *And So To Bed*: a day in the (hedonistic) life of diarist Samuel Pepys.

The week-long October production gave the Guild's reputation a much-needed boost and the appreciative audiences earned it a profit. Everyone breathed a sigh of relief.

Real life husband and wife – Philip and Joan Winter – were cast as Mr and Mrs Pepys and scored a hit with audiences and critics alike, the *Bromley & Kentish Times*, *Beckenham Journal* and *West Kent Mercury* all singling them out for colourful rhetoric.

Allan Holliday probably had the edge here.

'The actor plays the part throughout with verve, vigour and warm humanity; he speaks, moreover, with a strength and clarity which ensures that every word can be heard all over the theatre. Joan Winter is entirely captivating as Samuel's jealous wife. Never has this accomplished actress done anything better and the whole production's debt to her is immense'. Henry Graveney's sets were 'in the finest tradition' and costumes and props 'beyond reproach'.

St Mark's makes its debut

The year 1955 provided another landmark. An enthusiastic group of parishioners at St Mark's, Bromley got together to form a dramatic society which they subsequently named *St Mark's Players*.

The vicar who presided over that first meeting was invited to become president – a tradition that remains to this day.

Six months later the society staged its first play – *And This Was Odd* – which resulted in a profit of £15 10s, of which £9 10s was donated to the church hall fund.

At its first AGM the following year, *St Mark's* decided to allow guest producers into the group. It also agreed to join the Guild (but not to enter festivals until members had gained more experience!) A suggestion for a pantomime won general approval and *Aladdin and his Wonderful Lamp* (the first of many such enterprises) generated £20 for the church fund.

Monthly talks, play readings – even the odd jumble sale – featured in the *St Mark's* calendar and productions were increased from two to three per season. In 1960 the society entered its production of *The Chalk Garden* in the Kent Full Length Play Festival. It was the start of active festival participation with numerous awards and credits along the way.

Members also took part in the Guild's combined shows and manned a stall at the annual fair and fete.

Threat to future

No sooner had *St Mark's* celebrated its 21st birthday that news came of the parochial church council's decision to sell the church hall. The society's future was now under threat.

From left to right: Peggy Dallman, Teresa Williams, Reg Jackson and Robert Etherington in All of a Sudden Peggy *presented by* St Mark's Players *in 1974*
Photograph: Kentish Times

From left to right: John Ramsden, Paul Davies and Neil Scorgie in My Three Angels *presented by* Keston Amateur Dramatic Society *in the '50s*

Marjorie Waldron, who joined the group in 1970, recalls: 'I well remember the consternation over the fact that we weren't only going to lose the hall but also the outbuildings where we stored all our flats and equipment. Mercifully, Bromley Arts Council came to our aid and offered to give us temporary storage for our flats. The Saturday before the sale was spent transporting them all to the Arts Council's headquarters at Ripley. The lighting equipment was housed in the church gallery'.

The commitment to keep the society alive was strong and many permanent 'homes' were sought, mostly in vain. A production of *Woman in a Dressing Gown* (at Beckenham's Azelia Hall) won three awards in the Kent Festival and gave the society fresh heart.

Between 1955 and 1981 *St Mark's Players* presented 50 plays, 15 pantomimes and two music halls. Two long-time members, now dead, were wardrobe mistress Dora Coulson and Joan Dutton – one of the society's principal producers and a vice chairman of the Guild. In 1987 Croydon Advertiser critic Donald Madgwick asked Joan to produce his new play *The Year After the Fair* – a sequel to Frank Harvey's *The Day After the Fair* which Joan had produced in 1985. Joan was delighted to premiere the play.

In 1979 *St Mark's* booked Keston Village Hall – the home of *Keston Amateur Dramatic Society* – for *The Restless Evil*. At the time *Keston ADS* was about to fold due to lack of numbers so after the production the committees of both companies discussed the idea of collaborating on a joint venture. There were to be three joint productions before an inevitable – and successful – merger in the summer of 1981.

Since the merger, *St Mark's and Keston Players* have staged 38 plays, six music halls and one pantomime. A small nucleus of the original society still remains and links with St Mark's Church are retained as members rehearse in the new church room built in 1980.

Recent productions include *When We Are Married*, *Separate Tables*, *Man Alive*, *A Letter from the General*, *All the World's a Stage* and *The Vigil* (profits from which went to the church centenary fund which benefits three local charities: *Bromley Mencap's Blue Sky Appeal*, *Bromley Welcare* and *Bromley LATCH*).

In the spring of 1998 society member Michael Blake organised a series of drama workshops. These featured special exercises to develop articulation and projection; short scenes; stage grouping; solo speeches and extracts from classic and modern pieces. The workshops culminated in an evening's entertainment based on techniques studied.

From left to right: Michael Blake, Kara Tritton and Jill Cocovini in Gigi *presented by* St Mark's and Keston Players *in 1998*

Guild's first full length drama festival

In 1956 the Guild decided to upgrade its one-act play festival into a full length version which attracted six entries and was won by the *Green Room Club*.

Adjudicator Marjorie Herbert (founder of *Bromley Players*) commented on the high standard of the entries, saying that the 'bad old enemies of the amateur stage – the prompter and lack of rehearsal – were practically non-existent'. (The following year the festival was incorporated into the Kent Drama Festival).

Councillor Ralph Allen was elected Guild president in the same year, remaining in the post until his death in 1967.

The Guild's sixth show – in October 1965 – was Bayard Veiller's court room drama *The Trial of Mary Dugan* which was produced by Doris Burns at the *New Theatre*. Based on a real-life American trial of a famous showgirl in the early 20s, it featured the largest ever set at the *New* – 34 feet deep.

The American Embassy's legal department advised the producer on court procedure and to make sure the audience (who in fact formed the jury) entered into the spirit of the proceedings, American 'policemen' patrolled the foyer prior to the performance.

Veronica Harrison (of *The Curtain Raisers*) played the title role (with 'unusual polish', said the *Advertiser*) but much of the critical acclaim went to Jack Cockett (as the district attorney) and Alan Fleming (as Dugan's brother). Writing in the *Beckenham Journal*, David Shellan praised Cockett's 'marvellous accuracy and ferocious attack' and Fleming's 'accomplished and convincing performance'.

The production also marked a welcome return by Beryl Frisby – last seen in *Pomander Walk* despite the chest infection that put paid to any hopes of a professional acting career. Beryl played one of Dugan's showgirl colleagues.

Jack Cockett (right) in The Trial of Mary Dugan *presented by the Guild in 1956*

Chapter 6
Mixed Fortunes

The Guild staged two more shows in the 50s, the first of which was Anouilh's *Ring Round the Moon* in 1957. It was produced by W. Morgan Jones (from the *Glebe Knoll Players*) at the *New* and attracted a visit from Bromley's MP Harold Macmillan and his wife, Lady Dorothy.

As it turned out, Macmillan himself didn't make it until nearing the end of the show as he'd been delayed in the House but at the final curtain – accompanied by Councillor Ralph Allen – he climbed on to the stage to meet the cast.

In a brief address he traced the Guild's eight year history and said it was a 'wonderful tribute to the love of theatre in Bromley' that the town could support seven amateur dramatic societies – the number affiliated to the Guild at the time. He added: 'We have seen tonight a very polished performance in a play full of charm and whimsicality – not, I would imagine, a very easy play to act without great skill and knowledge'.

The critics didn't exactly agree with the Right Honourable Member for Bromley – the *West Kent Mercury* claimed the production needed 'far more attention to artistic detail than amateurs are able to provide' and the *Beckenham Advertiser* felt it was the kind of play 'they should leave well alone' – but individual performers fared well in the reviews – notably Henry Wooding.

Wooding played the double role of the identical twins and according to H.B. Hampton in the *Kentish Times* acted with 'immense zest, never muffing a single line of each of the two contrasting characters...a really brilliant performance'.

HBH also liked Pat Lee as Isabelle; Hilda Clarke as 'a witty old aristocrat'; Harold Armstrong as the butler; Joe Merrill as the millionaire and Bill Walker as the amorous butterfly-hunter.

And at the end of his review he gave a pat on the back to wardrobe mistresses Margaret Paice and Audrey Smith for the 'rich and beautiful' costumes.

Guild's eighth show

Almost exactly a year later came the Guild's eighth show – the 1958 production of Priestley's *When We Are Married*. The venue had moved to Bromley's Whitfield Hall and the producer was John Pett – an ex-member of the *New*'s repertory company and a drama critic for the *Croydon Advertiser*.

Pett was praised for a 'thorough, detailed but not fussy' interpretation of Priestley's farcical comedy about three couples celebrating their silver weddings who discover that the minister who married them was not technically authorised to do so!

H.B Hampton writing in the *Kentish Times* was complimentary about the acting. The three central couples (Bert Rogers, Edna Morris, Joe Stobart, Hilda Clarke, Bill Walker and Edna Newman) were 'straightforward, unexaggerated and convincing' and he singled out Alan Bardouleau's 'quiet and forceful' organist; Gertrude Westwood's 'admirably florid charwoman' and Sonia Rodway's 'amusing maidservant'.

There were backstage bouquets, too, for the 'wonderful setting' under the direction of Bill Lee; for Frank Maunder's impeccable stage management and lighting effects and for Ann Bunyan and Elizabeth Finch (in charge of props) who 'left nothing whatever to chance'.

Sixties bring problems for Guild

At the end of the year the roneo'd newsletter was dropped through lack of support and the Bromley Festival of 1959 attracted a mere five entries – a foretaste of the deeper problems that were to surface in 1961.

Conversely, local drama groups continued to flourish and the new decade brought three new names into the fold: the *Whitfield Players*; *Burnt Ash Drama Association* and *Theatre 62*.

In February 1960, 35 members of what was then Bromley Congregational Church in Widmore Road met under the chairmanship of the Minister (the Rev Eric Shave) and agreed to form a dramatic society. Its aim was to stage both religious and secular plays.

Taking its name from the church hall, the *Whitfield Players* (12 of its founder members were under 21) set about planning its first production – Agatha Christie's *Murder at the Vicarage* – which attracted an audience of 410 people at its two-night run and earned the society a triumphant £24.3.10d profit!

Two years later the hall was the venue for some 20 local churches of all denominations who joined forces with *Bromley Symphony Orchestra* and the *Ripley Choir* to present the *Chester Mystery Play Cycle*. (The event was described as 'unique and unrepeatable' but nonetheless found an echo 25 years later with the *National Theatre* version by the *Beta Players*).

In the 35 years of its existence (it folded in 1994) the *Whitfield Players* was loyal to its original aims but expanded its repertoire to include classical, modern, tragedy, comedy, thriller, farce, musical and two specially-devised revues for good measure. (By 1970 it was able to employ 36 cast members in a production of *Alice's Adventures in Wonderland*).

The cast of A Rose Without a Thorn *presented by the* Whitfield Players *in 1973*

A regular competitor in the Bromley Festival, the *Whitfield Players* won several acting prizes over the years as well as Best Lighting and Sound for *84 Charing Cross Road*, Best Stage Presentation for *Alphabetical Order* and Best Production for *Flowering Cherry*.

In the '80s, wherever possible, members endeavoured to contact authors of their productions and were rewarded by programme notes from Christopher Fry for *The Firstborn* and visits from Norman Ginsbury to *Viceroy Sarah* and Michael Green to *The Third Great Coarse Acting Show* (for which 23 actors played 64 roles!)

Perhaps the favourite piece of correspondence came from the late lamented Helene Hanff – the gutsy and immensely likeable author of *84 Charing Cross Road* (reproduced overleaf).

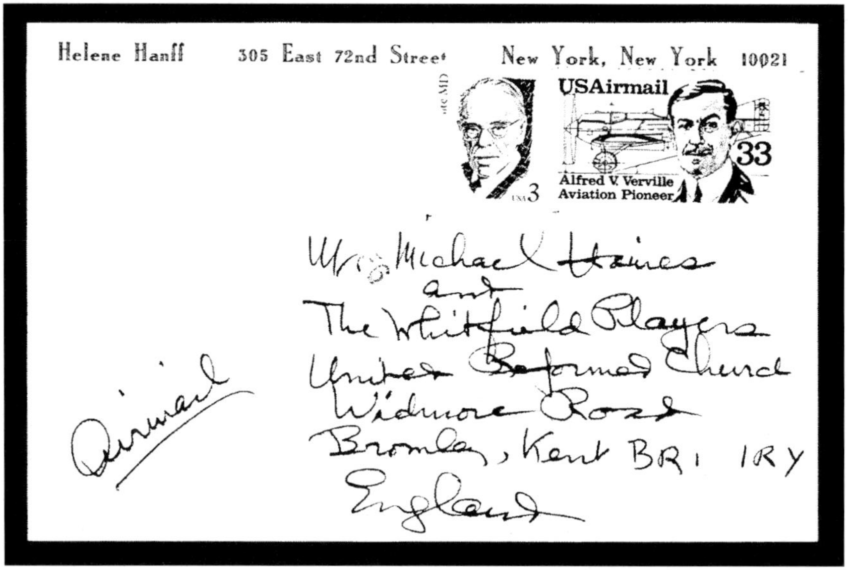
Helene Hanff 305 East 72nd Street New York, New York 10021

Mr. Michael Haines
and
The Whitfield Players
United Reformed Church
Widmore Road
Bromley, Kent BR1 1RY
England

Airmail

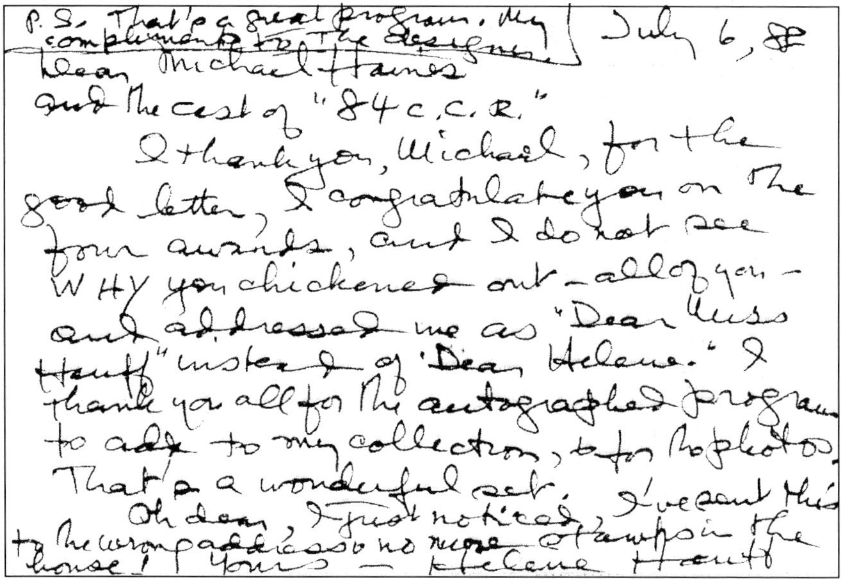
P.S. That's a great program. My compliments to the designer!

July 6, 88

Dear Michael Haines
and the cast of "84 C.C.R."

I thank you, Michael, for the good letter, I congratulate you on the four awards, and I do not see WHY you chickened out – all of you – and addressed me as "Dear Miss Hanff" instead of "Dear Helene." I thank you all for the autographed program to add to my collection, & for the photos. That's a wonderful set.

Oh dear, I just noticed, I've sent this to the wrong address so no more stamps in the house! Yours – Helene Hanff

For the benefit of those who find Ms Hanff's writing difficult to decipher it translates thus:

July 6, 88

Dear Michael Haines and the cast of '84 C.C.R.'

I thank you, Michael, for the good letter & congratulate you on the four awards, and I do not see WHY you chickened out – all of you – and addressed me as 'Dear Miss Hanff' instead of 'Dear Helene'. I thank you all for the autographed program to add to my collection, and for the photos. That's a wonderful set.

Oh dear, I just noticed, I've sent this to the wrong address & no more stamps in the house!

Yours – Helene Hanff

PS That's a great program. My compliments to the designer.

Alphabetical Order *presented by the* Whitfield Players *in 1992*

The society had a strong social calendar which incorporated essential fund-raising events – ultimately the popular 'Music Halls' which attracted a loyal and appreciative following.

In the early 90s the *Players* found themselves, in common with some other church-based groups, suffering a dearth of new members – especially younger people and those with technical skills. Standards were maintained (the *Kentish Times* reviewed the 1993 production of *Death of Salesman* as 'distinguished by an imposing set and particularly good performances) but at a cost – and in 1994 the committee decided to call a halt.

The society's swansong was *The Dresser* which won guest actor Steve Williams (former Guild chairman and now its Development Officer) Best Actor.

Members were active supporters of the Guild and provided two secretaries and its current chairman – Arthur Rochester: three times winner of the Festival's Best Actor award.

Guild's ninth show

The Guild chose Oscar Wilde's best loved comedy *The Importance of Being Earnest* for its ninth offering which its staged in June 1960. It was back to the *New* for the company, this time under the direction of Audrey Smith of the *Aperfield Players*.

It didn't make a profit and the reviews were mixed – 'workmanlike production' (*Kentish Times*); 'good try but too slow' (*Beckenham Advertiser*) – but it wasn't without its high spots.

Both papers were impressed by Hilda Clarke's Lady Bracknell; Bert Rogers' Canon Chasuble ('manna in the wilderness', said the *Advertiser*); Olive Davis' Miss Prism and Amy Cockett's production costumes which the *Advertiser* described as a 'tour de force from Miss Prism's jaunty boater and tie...to the charming grace of Cecily's roses'.

At the Guild's AGM the following March it was announced there would be no show in 1961. Instead, efforts would be concentrated on wiping out the outstanding deficit (about £80) on *The Importance of Being Earnest.*

Member societies were criticised for doing 'too little in the way of selling tickets'. (As it turned out it would be another three years before the Guild staged its next show).

By the 1962 AGM the financial situation had improved – there was now a net profit of £13 10s 10d – and the Guild shortened its name to *Bromley Theatre Guild.*

Making its mark

Meanwhile, the Bromley-based *St Andrew's Dramatic Society* (later to be renamed *Burnt Ash Drama Association*) was beginning to make its mark.

The arrival of a new choirmaster and his wife at the church in 1961 was to have far-reaching consequences in matters non-religious, so to speak.

The once flourishing drama group had

The Importance of Being Earnest *presented by the Guild in 1960*

disbanded due to lack of support but Pamela Warwick proved an inspirational force – not just in getting it back on its feet but in helping the new society build a reputation for challenging theatre.

By 1967 the inadequacies of St Andrew's hall forced a much-needed removal to St Augustine's hall in Grove Park where the society continued to flourish under its mentors – not least St Andrew's curate, Colin Oxenforth.

The production of A *Streetcar Named Desire*

From left to right: Vera Kemp, Cyril Wallace, Pam Warwick, William Burford and Shirley Lock in Quiet Weekend *presented by* St Andrew's DS *(now* BADA*) – the society's first production in 1961*

in 1975 proved another turning point. Most importantly, it won the Bromley Festival and came third in the Kent Festival – but looking back it seems more than coincidence that the decision followed soon after to change the society's name to *Burnt Ash Drama Association*.

Writing in St Andrew's magazine at the time, Bill Burford (another of the group's driving forces) was anxious to stress that the change of name in no way implied a desire 'to break away from the church'. The reasons were to end the confusion between St Andrew's and St Augustine's and to widen the society's scope.

A year later the group returned to its old stamping ground of St Andrew's hall – subsequently refurbished, making local drama history in 1977 with the first full-length play in St Andrew's Church – *The Roses of Eyam* – involving a cast of 50.

Minack connection

BADA's 16-year association with Cornwall's famous open air theatre *The Minack* began in 1978 with a production of *She Stoops to Conquer*. It was cast from *BADA* members and friends but all future productions drew on additional resources from the *Whitfield Players* and *Theatre 62*.

There is justifiable regret that the society no longer performs there – the result of a decision by the Minack management to invite either professional companies or large amateur groups with more of a 'name'.

Minack's formidable founder Rowena Cade (who died in 1983) was a passionate supporter of amateur groups and is remembered with affection by *BADA* members.

'On each first night she always sent a tray of peaches down to the dressing room, together with a little note, with good wishes', says Andrea Gambell. 'She could often be seen sitting in an upturned wheelbarrow at the top of a cliff'.

The society has made two Spanish appearances – at the Teatro Salon Varietes in Fuengirola – in 1988 with *Outside Edge* and in 1996 with *A Country Wife*. (The theatre is run by an enthusiastic committee of ex-pats and houses local amateur drama and operatic groups).

In July 1998 *BADA* revived their open-air tradition by presenting *A Midsummer Night's Dream* in Church House Gardens behind the Churchill Theatre. Directed by Dennis Bradley (who played Puck in *BADA*'s 1980 Minack production), it featured members of the Churchill Theatre Youth Section and other young performers.

In an attempt to make some profit on each production, *BADA* has introduced bar facilities, thanks to the support of its local pub *The Prince Frederick* in Nichol Lane.

'We are indebted to the landlord Greg Weall and his predecessor Simon Penney', says Andrea Gambell.

Minack 1992 – A Man for All Seasons *presented by* BADA

BADA has won Bromley Festival on six occasions and collected numerous other Festival awards over the years.

...In 1973, however, things didn't go quite so well for *St Andrew's DS* who incurred the wrath of the Bromley Festival adjudicator with its production of *A Man for All Seasons*.

Mr Percy Steven said he was very angry when companies deviated from the playwright's script.

'You are creative interpreters and must not change a word', he added.

Enter *Theatre 62*

As its name implies, *Theatre 62* was founded in 1962 – a logical merger of two existing groups with individual strengths: *West Wickham Amateur Dramatic Society* and *The Actories* which evolved from the Conservative Association.

The move was to prove very successful but in those early days not without its difficulties, as founder member Bill Taylor recalls.

'We suddenly found we had two of everything – two chairmen, two secretaries and two names! Finally, Roland Oliver – a professional actor and a member – suggested *Theatre 62* so we gave him a life membership'.

Theatre 62's first production was *Watch It, Sailor* – the somewhat lack-lustre sequel to *Sailor Beware* – but in the years to come the repertoire was to include many more demanding pieces such as *The Tempest*, *Twelfth Night*, *Arms and the Man*, *Under Milk Wood*, *She Stoops to Conquer*, *Ritual for Dolls*, *The Diary of Anne Frank*, *Cider with Rosie*, *A Voyage Round My Father*, *Wuthering Heights* and *Cat on a Hot Tin Roof* – many of which won awards.

Prior to moving into its own clubhouse, *Theatre 62*'s regular venue was Wickham Hall. Long-time member Phyllis Mortimer – a doctor who retired to Seaford three years ago – remembers the 'tunnel' that went under the stage. 'Actors have been known to collide in this tunnel while hurrying in opposite directions, neither knowing which side was his next entrance. No names but Sir Toby Belch and Sir Andrew Aguecheek will know who I mean!' Phyllis' husband Jack, also an active member, has his own memories of the venue. During an unforgettable performance of Dylan Thomas' *The Doctor and the Devils* he was required, as narrator, to ad lib a la Thomas while the actors playing body snatchers Burke and Hare struggled with a body-sized box that had got stuck in the tunnel!

Acquisition of the theatre centre in Corkscrew Hill – the former rugby football clubhouse – was the realisation of a long-cherished dream by the members who planned its transformation. Chaired by Will Howells, the 262 Club worked unstintingly to raise funds for the project which had only been achieved, he said at the official launch in October 1972, by 'a lot of strife, trouble and argument'!

When the group moved into its new home there was no Green Room. The company was lent a 'shaky, worn and very small' caravan for the purpose where the frequent cry from the actors was 'stand still please I'm doing my eye-liner', says Sheila Rudderham.

After the floor of the caravan collapsed the green room moved to a builder's hut – smaller still and without heating.

Braving the elements in the 50yard sprint between the Green Room and backstage is never easy ('particularly in a howling gale dressed in elegant 19th century ball dresses and satin slippers', adds Sheila) – and such vagaries have prompted a lottery application for funds to build an extension.

Seasoned award winners (since 1979 it has won Bromley Festival on six occasions) and participators in a variety of festivals, the club welcomes the friendly rivalry even if it doesn't always agree with the adjudicator!

Bill Taylor again: 'In 1971 we entered *She Stoops to Conquer* in the Bromley Festival. The newspaper critics were all praise but the adjudicator Rolf Kruger was overall far more critical. The only person he really seemed to like was Carolyn (Taylor's wife). Most of the cast, having listened at the back of the stage, wandered back to the Green Room muttering things like "Oh well, we've had that…" As it happened, he placed us second to *Hayes Players* with Carolyn winning Best Actress'

Theatre 62 has always had a theatre cat. Bootsie and Smudge (the latter is still alive but very ancient!) adopted the unnerving habit of wandering on stage at certain performances – a trait shared by the slick, black Tituba named after the black servant girl in *The Crucible*. She was often to be found snoozing on a sofa during a show but her *piece de resistance* was in *The Trial of Mary Dugan*. Says Audrey Smithard: 'The night the adjudicator attended, Tituba spent the performance asleep on a "policeman"'s lap. When he praised her at the awards ceremony, on hearing her name, tail held high she walked straight up the centre aisle, mounted the stage and acknowledged her applause!'

Interaction with other Guild members occasionally leads to joint ventures such as the chance to join with *Burnt Ash Drama Association* in its production of *A Man For All Seasons* at the Minack Theatre in Cornwall in 1992.

'The thrill, fun and excitement of those two weeks will never fade', says chairman of the production committee, Brenda Noble – a founder

From left to right: Anne John, Mary Grimwood, Laura Byers, Jean Golder and Joy Judd in John Snow *presented by* Theatre 62 *in 1994*

member who was originally a member of *The Actories*.

Another founder member Jim Judd, who played at Minack, recalls: 'On any stage, projection is all. At the Minack, more so. There the audience ascends almost to the heavens with one section seated up a kind of gully which can give the actors an unsettling feeling of being

From left to right: Claire Morris, Rosemary Harris, Alec Raemers and Dennis Packham in Wuthering Heights *presented by* Theatre 62 *in 1996*

critically appraised virtually from behind'.

Many *Theatre 62* members have been involved in Guild productions. Among them are husband and wife Ray and Rosemary Harris (whose associations with *Bromley Players* are recalled elsewhere in the book). Ray was a teacher at Hayes School from whom the club has recruited a number of its younger members. Both have received awards for acting and directing.

The Harris' have a fund of anecdotes such as the night Ray (playing Nelson) sent his leading lady's wig flying into the wings during a romantic scene in *Bequest to the Nation* (1978) and the moment when one of Rosemary's props caused her acute embarrassment in *The Mysteries* (1987).

'I had to carry an old-fashioned water bottle in a string bag. To make things look "period", the props lady had inserted a wedge of paper in the bottle before filling it with water. In one scene I had to kneel and pray. On rising, a large puddle was visible on the stage floor and my lower garments were decidedly damp!'

It's perhaps appropriate to mention in this chapter that in 1951 four West Wickham societies formed the *West Wickham Theatre Guild*. Founding groups were *West Wickham Dramatic Society*, *Wickham Court Players* (now *New Wickham Court Players*), *West Wickham Operatic Society* and the *Boleyn Players* (now extinct). Later the *Kismet Players* (also now extinct) joined the Guild but unfortunately it didn't survive the years.

The Ray Bardell Trophy for Bromley Festival's sound and lighting award was presented by *Theatre 62* in 1984 in memory of an active member and former chairman.

Chapter 7
Time Moves On

Three years had now elapsed since the last Guild show but in 1964 Ben Levy's mythological frolic *The Rape of the Belt* put it back on the performing map in a production at Hayes Village Hall.

Levy's play creates considerable headaches for the producer who has to decide whether it is simply a debunking of the classical tradition or a modern morality play.

Audrey Smith opted for a comedy of manners and played it strictly for laughs.

For the most part it paid off and Donald Madgwick, writing in the *Beckenham Advertiser*, commented: 'The pace was brisk, the voices firm and audible and the groupings had a quality of naturalness and simplicity that wedded them firmly to the text'.

Rosemary Harris' Antiope, Patricia Lee's Hippolyte, Betty Strike's Hera and Bert Rogers' Zeus caught his eye particularly.

One scene from the play is etched indelibly on Rosemary's mind. The costume department had hired a real lion skin for the unfortunate Heracles (Denis Hitchcock) who only had a few hours practice before staggering on stage in it on the first night.

The Waltz of the Toreadors *presented by the Guild in 1965*

The Rape of the Belt *presented by the Guild in 1964.*
Photograph: Kentish Times

Ann Veronica *presented by the Guild in 1966*

'What the wardrobe mistress hadn't told him was the claws were real', says Rosemary. 'A welcome sit-down on an inviting stage boulder with a claw in entirely the wrong position saw a vaulting Heracles rise to the height of the Gods!'

Audrey Smith's third show for the Guild – Anouilh's *The Waltz of the Toreadors* – was presented at Hayes Village Hall in 1965.

Ray and Rosemary Harris played the General and his wife and the first night evokes more memories from the Harris anecdotes. Says Rosemary: 'Just before curtain up the stage manager had decided to substitute the bedspread on the double bed for one made of rather slippery satin. During an angry exchange in one of the scenes I had to leap onto the bed – and immediately slid to the floor!'

H.G. Wells centenary

In 1966 the Guild became an integral part of the newly-founded Bromley Arts Council from which it receives an annual grant which helps subsidise the Bromley Festival.

That same year – to mark the H.G.Wells Centenary – the Guild staged Wells' satirical piece on the suffragette movement: *Ann Veronica*. The producer was Katheryn Scott of the Central School of Speech and Drama.

The *Kentish Times* praised the production's 'real feeling for the Edwardian era', paying tribute to both producer and stage director John Townsend for their clever use of an apron stage.

In the title role Rosemary Harris displayed 'true stagecraft'; Audrey Smith played Ann's confidante, Miss Klegg, with 'particular understanding' and Gertrude Westwood scored highly (again!) as the priceless landlady. 'This was acting which conveyed quite perfectly the I-know-my-place-but-the-upper-class-must-have-their-fun attitude of the bottle of stout in the kitchen brigade'. Backstage tributes went to Amy Cockett for the costumes and Hugh Marley and Cyril Connor for the impressive sound effects.

Can I have my bucket back?

Mentioning backstage tributes brings to mind the subject of props...Delving in the Guild's archives I have unearthed all manner of gems – some printable; some not. The following caught my attention – partly because it highlights the unenviable task of the person in charge of the props but mostly because the author took the trouble to entertain the reader.

From a secretary's postbag....

Dear *(name witheld to protect the innocent)*

Please do not take this letter personally. I am writing to you as secretary, not as yourself.

I am not a mean person. Any of my friends will confirm that. If you asked me for a £10 donation I would give gladly; if you doubled the subscription I wouldn't bat an eyelid; if you asked for a bucket I'd buy one – indeed, I'd willingly buy 10 buckets.

However, I recently lent the society a bucket and when I LEND something I expect it returned in the same condition as I last saw it.

It was not, as some people have suggested, my responsibility to collect the bucket after the play. It was the responsibility of whoever did the 'props' to keep a proper list of what was lent, and by whom, and see it was returned.

In short, I have lost a white, heat-resistant two gallon bucket calibrated in gallons and litres and I expect the society either to return or (if necessary) replace it.

Regards,

Link with the past

Ralph Allen's death in 1967 severed a link with the past. He had been Guild chairman since 1950 – a role he had combined with that of president since Colonel B.J. 'Bunjie' Finnie had resigned on health grounds in 1956. Allen had also been a chairman and president of *Hayes Players* and was last mayor of Bromley before the creation of the London Borough of Bromley. Dorothy Marriott was elected president and Allan Holliday chairman.

There was no Guild show that year (nor the following) but at the Bromley Arts Council's quarterly meeting in February 1969 plans were unveiled for an amateur theatre which would seat 300. The estimated cost was between £20,000 and £30,000 and it was scheduled for 1970.

Hopes were high and in the programme for the Guild's 21st birthday production – Ronald Gow's comedy *The Edwardians* at the *New Theatre* in 1970 – Allan Holliday spoke about the playhouse project under the leadership of the late Cliff Russell in very positive terms.

The *Beckenham Advertiser* praised producer Gerald Williams (the Guild's first chairman) for 'a firm hand and a clear eye' in his interpretation of *The Edwardians* and spoke of the high standards; excellent set and costumes and painstaking attention to detail with regard to props.

Hayes Player Elisabeth Hyams, who played the Duke's mother, remembers the production with affection – despite some nerve-wracking moments.

'One of the reasons is because the *New Theatre* burned down not long afterwards and some unkind individuals placed the blame on me for jinxing the place which I strongly deny! In fact I thought it was rather a horrid theatre, complete with deaf spots in the auditorium, and one member of the audience actually took the trouble to come round during the interval to inform me he was unable to catch a single word.

'Rehearsing *Edwardians* was a delight but the producer didn't pull any punches. One day he shouted at me: "Oh God you're so middle-class". I was completely demoralised by this remark and stammered: "Is it my accent?" to which he replied: "Oh no, your voice is fine – it's just you!".

'After this episode I worked very hard on being upper-crust, becoming more and more imperious, snobbish and arrogant day by day. In time the whole thing was second nature. My poor husband remarked that he was rather tired of living with the Duchess and if I didn't tone it down a bit he would be leaving home!

'After it was all over the producer thanked me for giving such a lovely performance, adding: "You didn't do a single thing I asked you but thank you all the same"'.

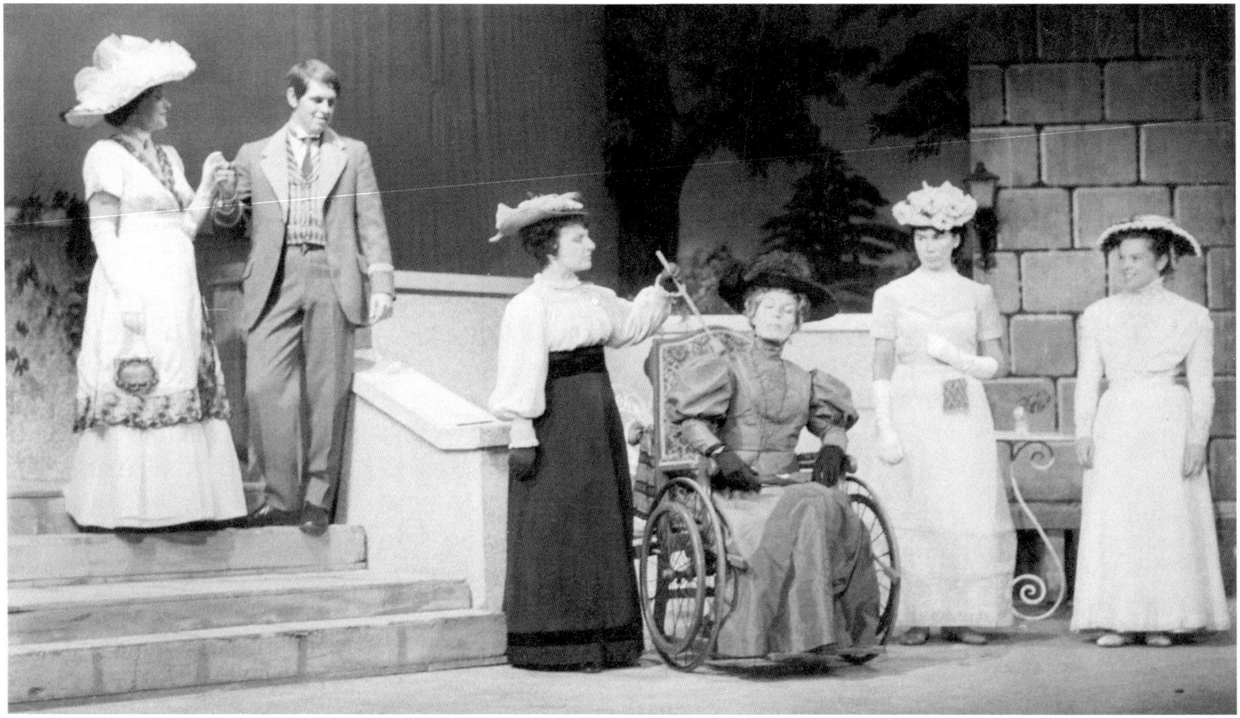

The Guild's 21st birthday production in 1970: The Edwardians

Spirits sag

The production made a loss of £200 and spirits sagged. 'Hardly the way to collect funds for an amateur theatre in Bromley', lectured the reinstated Guild newsletter in October 1970. The February 1971 newsletter recorded slow progress on the project due to lack of funds and asked member societies to look out for suitable sites or possible conversions.

The debate would continue, resurfacing in the June 1972 newsletter when Stan Mole reported a certain amount of cynicism among societies as to the project's chances of success. He said the committee was investigating the new hall to be built in Orpington.

By February 1974 he wrote: 'The Guild remains as homeless as an itinerant pedlar. Its meetings are held in decaying Denmark Villas and it inhabits briefly the gracious rooms of *Ripley* for the odd drama event and rehearsal but it belongs nowhere.

'The acquisition of a small hall for conversion into a Guild Club seems to me to be a first step towards the establishment of a great ideal that has yet to be realised. Have we been looking down the wrong end of a telescope in talking of grandiose schemes to build an amateur theatre?'

More of the debate in a later chapter. Meanwhile, when the *New* burned down in May 1971 the Guild lost its venue for the profitable annual Music Halls devised in 1966 in association with the *BADS* under the direction of John Hurst.

Masterly show

The Guild's masterly 1972 show – Coward's pageant *Cavalcade* – involved 20 member societies. It was the first amateur production of the play and its producer – Peter Hahlo – was recommended by the *Advertiser* critic Donald Madgwick.

'I suggested Peter Hahlo', says Madgwick, 'because he was a gifted man of the theatre whose work in his own Surrey area was widely admired and *Cavalcade* – which employs a huge cast in spanning the first three decades of this century – was the sort of challenge to which the Guild was always happy to respond.

'I wrote of the production: "This was more than a director's showpiece: it was a splendid advertisement for the combined talents of the score or so of societies comprising the Bromley Theatre Guild. Having followed most of these societies over the years, I was only confirmed in my opinion that the district contains a splendid reservoir of ability"'.

The amount of music written specially for the show was relatively small – the famous *20th Century Blues* number of the prologue, the 1930 night club scene and a handful of songs representing an excerpt from a 1900 musical comedy, the best known of which was *Lover of My Dreams*.

However, there is a wealth of music of the period – 1899–1930 – which includes the popular songs of the Boer War and the 1914–18 War as well as those of 1906 and 1910. In all it amounts to a grand total of 37 songs ranging from *Dolly Gray* to *My Old Man*, *The Merry Widow* waltz, *Keep the Home Fires Burning*, *Beside the Seaside* and *Alexander's Ragtime Band*.

John Hurst was responsible for compiling the musical score and providing the piano accompaniment. Asked what he thought of such a challenge he replied: 'I'm enjoying it immensely – who wouldn't with a producer of Peter Hahlo's ability and such a talented cast?'

Margaret Cronk has already described her panic at being responsible for the 200 costumes for the 42 members of the cast (in the first chapter) but Vicky Purnell, Alice Attwood and Amy Cockett were on hand for support. David Waterhouse (of *Beckenham Theatre Centre*) designed the sets to leave the maximum stage space while depicting the passage of time. Jane Janes proved a skilful stage director.

A scene from the Guild's 1970 production of Cavalcade

Ambitious venture

The following June, Howard Richardson and William Berney's eerie play of the occult, *Dark of the Moon* attracted considerable press attention. It was a deliberately ambitious venture on the part of the Guild for its 1973 showcase, following, as it did, in the wake of the popular *Cavalcade* whose high standards were to set a precedent for the rest of the decade.

Stephen Morant directed the production (at Orpington Civic Hall) and whet a lot of theatrical appetites in an interview he did with the *Kentish Times*.

'It's a play full of all the elements which make drama a living art', he said. 'There is love, hate, empathy, high drama, low comedy – in all, a perfect profile of a superstitious rural American community at the turn of the century, bedevilled by their fears and fantasies and totally immersed in their loves and hates'.

Strong stuff – but Morant was no innocent in the business of publicity. *Guildhall School of Music and Drama* trained (he won the Memorial Prize for the best results of the year), he was performer as well as director and *Dark of the Moon* was his 30th production in four years.

In his review for the *Advertiser*, Donald Madgwick thought the production 'an eloquent testimony to the strength of theatre in the district…strongly fuelled from within and something of a triumph'.

Richard Hutton's witch boy was a performance of 'huge magnetism' – well matched by Mair Lloyd-Roberts 'fire and fervour' as Barbara – and there were commendations for Ray Harris' 'almost Satanic' Preacher Haggler; William Burford's 'laconic' Mr Allen; Ken Richardson's 'folksy' Uncle Smelicue and Hedley Brook-Carter's 'smoulderingly resentful' Marvin Hudgens.

Cliff Russell gave much the same assessment in the *Kentish Times* – 'a show of contrasts, the expertise with which it was endowed as good as last year (*Cavalcade*) and deserving of much better support'.

Prior to the show's first night, Russell had interviewed stage director Jane Janes, describing her as 'an indefatigable worker' whose interest in stage management had been triggered when she deputised for a colleague at *St Mark's Players* who was taken ill.

Jane was involved in many Guild productions as well as those for the *North West Kent Federation of Townswomen's Guilds* and *The Marlowe Society*.

She told Russell: 'I keep trying to retire but to no avail!'

Cliff Russell's own involvement with the Guild had begun in 1952 when he temporarily deserted *Eltham Little Theatre* where he was stage director to become joint production manager (with Gerald Williams) for *Twelfth Night*.

Guild's Silver Jubilee year

In its Silver Jubilee year – 1974 – the Guild (by now a charity) had 27 member societies.

Clearly, the occasion called for an ambitious project and Joan Macalpine's adaptation of Henry Fielding's rumbustious Restoration romp *Tom Jones* proved a popular choice at Orpington Civic Hall.

Producer Ron Tinker – who had been involved in amateur productions, as performer and director, for 30 years – was applauded for his 'meticulous' (if slightly overlong) production which required his cast to abandon restraint and enter into the spirit of the thing with lascivious energy.

Edna Walker elicited a glowing comment from Cliff Russell in the *Kentish Times* for her 'superb interpretation of the slatternly Mrs Mop' and he reckoned Dorothy Locke 'delightfully expressive' as Molly – one of Tom's early conquests.

Dorothy, as it happens, had taken the auditions for the show very seriously, enhancing the assets nature had bestowed on her by wearing a 'wonderbra' for the occasion.

'I got the part and was at a costume fitting one evening when Ron walked in. When he realised who I was he said: "I cast you because you had a voluptuous bosom. Where's it gone?". Of course I hadn't got 'the bra' on but they managed to fix things for the production!'

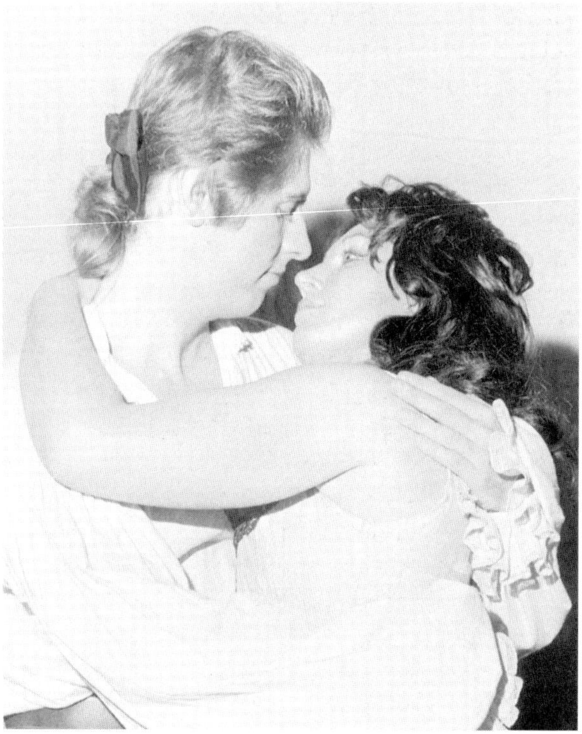

Peter Sowerbutts as Tom and Dorothy Locke as Molly in Tom Jones *presented by the Guild in 1974*

Peter Sowerbutts played Tom and Dorothy recalls a dramatic first night when, following director's orders, she duly ruffled her leading man's hair in suggestive fashion. 'The only problem was that the make-up person hadn't told me she'd sprayed hair lacquer on him before his entrance. We played the scene with Peter's hair sticking up on end!'

Moments of glory

Feydeau's *Cat Among the Pigeons* is far from his best farce (even with John Mortimer's witty translation) but the Guild's 1975 version directed by Ron Tinker at Orpington Civic Hall had its moments of glory.

In his review for the *Advertiser*, Donald Madgwick dwelled, in particular, on Ken Richardson's portrayal of the Mexican General Irrigua. 'Conceived to outsize proportions', he wrote, 'the performance shone with that grotesque exaggeration of realistic traits by which classic farce makes its mark'.

There was praise, too, for the 'lazy charm and vast appetite for intrigue' of Peter Sowerbutts' Bois d'Enghien; Brian Etheridge's Ignace (played with 'comic gusto') and Bob Miles' idiosyncratic Bouzin. Edna Walker, he pointed out, only needed a more artificial manner to make her 'sparkle like a Christmas tree'. (I wonder what the actress made of that.)

Churchill connection

One of the Guild's 'youngest' member societies is the *Churchill Theatre Youth Section – CTYS –* which was formed in 1977 after its 'parent' theatre opened in the July of that year.

Students are admitted on a first-come, first-served basis rather than through auditions and previous experience and current membership is around 100.

There are three categories – Juniors (seven to 11);

Ken Richardson and Edna Walker in the Guild's 1975 production of Cat Among the Pigeons

Inters (11–14) and Seniors (14–18) – all of which are encouraged to take part in the company's regular productions.

A member of the Guild since 1989, *CTYS* enjoys a challenge. In 1990, through its association with the *National Operatic and Dramatic Association* (*NODA*), it was invited to take part in the Queen Mother's 90th birthday celebrations – an event students will never forget. QM90 was held on Horse Guards Parade in London.

Later that year *NODA* awarded the company the Constance Power Trophy for the society most worthy of encouragement following its memorable production of *The Snow Queen* presented at the *Churchill* as part of *Bromley Borough Arts Festival*.

Thanks to generous sponsorship from Natwest Bank, *CTYS* was able to mount an adventurous production of Peter Schaffer's *Amadeus* in the 1991 Bromley Festival.

Playing Mozart was Simon Grieff who won the Best Actor Under 21 award and later turned professional. (He has recently received favourable reviews in the London Palladium production of *Saturday Night Fever*).

At one point the production was in danger of being cancelled, recalls Administrator Christine Howell: 'Students started coming down with chickenpox but fortunately we managed to carry on somehow. *Amadeus* was directed by David Evans who, later in the same Festival, won Best Actor in a Major Role for his performance in *Burnt Ash Drama Association*'s winning production of *Molly*. The adjudicator commented particularly on David's make-up, saying she was most impressed by the way he had made himself look so revoltingly spotty. Little did she realise that he had caught chickenpox and the spots were real!'

Simon Grieff as Mozart and Chloe Spencer as Constanze in CTYS's *1991 production of* Amadeus

The company also took part in the Guild's reinstated one act play festivals at Bromley's Whitfield Hall in 1993, 1994 and 1995.

At a special Youth Night in 1993, 27 juniors presented *Beowulf* devised by Peter Jolly, Barbara Vousden and the company. Both the plot and the action were developed through improvisation and workshop sessions. It earned a special mention from the assessor who commented: 'The company works excellently together and the show is a first class example of ensemble theatre'.

In July 1998 *CTYS* staged *The Adventures of Alice* by Bill Morley and Pamela Turnlund in Church House Gardens, Bromley in association with *BADA*. Based on Lewis Carroll's *Alice in Wonderland* and *Alice Through the Looking Glass*, the production marked the centenary of Carroll's death.

Vivat! Vivat Regina!

Donald Madgwick and I both agreed that Stephen Morant's interpretation of Robert Bolt's rather wordy *Vivat! Vivat Regina!* in 1977 (ideas were scrapped for the Guild's 1976 production) was overlong and in need of some judicious pruning.

That said, this story of the two Renaissance queens, Elizabeth Tudor and Mary Stuart, holds an inevitable fascination and this production at

Orpington Civic Hall yielded some exceptional acting – notably Mair Lloyd-Roberts as the capricious Mary.

'Finely studied and beautifully spoken performance', said Madgwick; 'one of the most moving and expressive characterisations of the evening' (my verdict). I was also much taken with Brian McEwan's Bothwell, I remember.

Madgwick described Edna Walker as 'a living embodiment of Tudor arrogance' as Elizabeth, her transformation from young woman to imperious despot 'truly astonishing'. Other commended cast members were Arthur Rochester as Cecil; William Burford as Walsingham and Ken Richardson as John Knox.

The wardrobe team, headed by Margaret Cronk, was its usual meticulous self.

Smaller-scale

The Guild show for 1978 – Terrence Rattigan's *Bequest to the Nation* (produced by Rosemary Harris) – was a smaller-scale affair and saw a change of venue from Orpington to Hayes Village Hall.

Rattigan's play tells of the short period immediately before the Battle of Trafalgar in October 1805 when a sick and battle-weary Nelson is torn between his devotion to the duty England expected of him and his dependence on his mistress, Emma Hamilton.

Elisabeth Hyams played Emma to Ray Harris' Nelson and she recalls the fun she had in portraying 'the vulgar, over-blown tippler' of Rattigan's creation which gave her plenty of scope for a bit of ham acting! (The *Advertiser* commented: 'Looking like one of Rowlandson's fat Regency ladies, she was splendidly hammy, regaling all and sundry with a stream of coarse epithets'.)

Things didn't always go according to plan on stage, however.

'One night when I was seated at the harpsichord I suddenly rose and the harpsichord went on playing', says Rosemary. 'I hastily resumed my seat but too late…the audience had a good titter at that little lapse! On another occasion, while whirling round striking one of the character's famous attitudes, I accidentally caught my attendant maid a tremendous swipe round the side of her head, nearly braining the poor girl'.

Ray Harris' memory of dislodging Emma's wig is documented in Chapter 6!

Ray Harris and Elisabeth Hyams in the Guild's production of Bequest to the Nation *in 1978*

CHAPTER 8
Taking Stock

Leafing through the Guild's newsletters of the time reveals that Allan Holliday was elected president in 1979, succeeding the late Dorothy Marriott, and Graham Finch retired as chairman.

In an earlier newsletter Finch had produced an interesting appraisal of the Guild, having been asked to comment on its future by the newsletter Editor, Stan Mole (later to succeed him as chairman).

'If there were no Guild there would still be a number of individual Bromley societies doing very well' wrote Finch. 'The Guild was invented by a collection of gentlemen who – rightly – saw that it could serve a useful purpose. But having invented it, that doesn't mean that all societies need it. Needs are so dissimilar that it would require something far larger than the Guild to cope with them all. The Guild means different things to different people and, in the final analysis, totally lacks the authority and disciplines of the constituent societies. 'To face facts, a considerable number of actors and actresses couldn't care less if the Guild disappeared tomorrow. However, having said all that, I consider drama in Bromley is in a healthier state because of its existence'.

And touching on a sensitive issue, he urged that one of the Guild's priorities should be the acquisition of rehearsal and storage space. 'That does not mean I consider a theatre an unworthy ambition but I think we have to take a long hard look at priorities'.

Editor retires

Prior to his election as chairman, Stan Mole (who has been involved in a number of Guild societies) stood down as newsletter Editor after several years in the post. Paying tribute to his efforts, Cliff Russell, by now vice president, touched on another sore subject – apathy.

Said Russell: 'Stan has been a competent and painstaking Editor under far from congenial circumstances. That his valuable contributions to the Guild have not been properly recognised seem evident to me and although he pleads pressure of other interests as the cause of his resignation I suspect members' apathy concerning the newsletter is the main reason'.

This was not his first outspoken comment on the subject.Three years earlier in the newsletter he had railed against members' lack of support, questioning why many 'workable schemes and progressive ideas' had been swept under the carpet.

New decade

The new decade would see the launch of a new society (*The Matchbox Theatre*) and yet another appeal by Stan Mole for an amateur theatre. But in 1980 these events were still in the future. First came the Guild's show – Lionel Bart's ever-popular musical *Oliver!* – which was produced by Jeffrey Smith at Orpington Civic Hall.

It was a production full of energy and enthusiasm (I know because I read my review!) and Smith had disciplined his large cast admirably well, eliciting a string of excellent performances from Ray Harris' Fagin and Dorothy Locke's Nancy to Matthew Pateman's Oliver, Paul Glynn's Artful Dodger and Arthur Rochester and Rosemary Harris' Mr Bumble and Widow Corney.

There was little to dislike – certainly not an atmospheric set by Sally Langford and attractive choreography (Barbara Sowerbutts). In the chorus were students of *Les Jeunes Dramatistes* – an acting class run by Pat Hammond at Ripley. (Pat's late husband John – mentioned elsewhere in this book – was stage director).

Guild's youngest society

The Guild's youngest society – *The Matchbox Theatre* – was founded in 1981 and is affiliated to St Francis Church, West Wickham where most of its productions are performed. It gets its name from the size of the stage in the church hall – relatively unused prior to the group's activities.

Since its debut production – *The Happiest Days of Your Life* (directed by Pat Williams and featuring church members of all ages and acting abilities) – *The Matchbox* has gone from strength to strength, acquiring a reputation for both the quality and diversity of its challenging repertoire.

In 1984, the vicar of St Francis – Jack Webb – retired. The committee held its breath. He had been a great friend and champion of the little theatre and could always be relied upon to wake up the Thursday night audiences by guffawing loudly from the back of the hall.

The state of interregnum dragged on for two years and then *The Matchbox* struck gold – in the shape of the Rev Canon Owen Everson. On the last leg of his career before retirement (and with acting in his blood), he arrived – with his wife Nadja – at St Francis and accepted the position of honorary president with good grace.

With a little gentle coaxing from his churchwarden Pat Williams, he began to take on small roles when time and his other 'roles' permitted.

Under Everson's patronage the group even used the church itself for the occasional production – notably in 1991 with the unusual play *The Gut Girls* which is set in an abattoir. This had its drawbacks, however, as Vicky Pearce explains:

Owen Everson as Starveling in A Midsummer Night's Dream *presented by* The Matchbox Theatre *in 1994*
Photo: Captured Images

'Thanks to Paul Johnson, an acting member and local butcher, real meat was used for the play. One member of the cast – Chris Morgan –was pregnant at the time and found the whole business of handling the raw, and gradually "turning" cuts of offal, difficult – to say the least. Every night Paul took the meat back to his freezer, returning it the following day (neither Paul's nor *The Matchbox*'s budget could stretch to fresh cuts each night). By the Sunday morning service – after two dress rehearsals and three performance nights – the church was not really a very nice place to be!'

Memorable performances

Everson retired at Easter 1998 with several memorable performances under his belt – shocking some of his parishioners by appearing to relieve himself in the bushes as Starveling in *A Midsummer Night's Dream* and using language not considered appropriate for a man of the cloth as Moon in *The Real Inspector Hound*, to name but two!

His last role was as Fabian in the 1996 production of *Twelfth Night* but in 1998 he and Nadja journeyed from their new home in Chichester to support *The Taming of the Shrew*.

In 1994 the group's treasurer Tim Pearce persuaded members they should present an open-air production of *A Midsummer Night's Dream* in aid of charity. And so the *Normanhurst* tradition began.

This large house in Bishops Walk, Croydon (which belongs to John and Pat Williams) was the ideal venue for such a venture and the production – which also involved other Guild members (principally *Hayes Players*) – was staged in the front garden.

Audiences were invited to picnic in the grounds – à la Glyndebourne; grandstands and marquees were hired and the event was sponsored by the Rotary Club of Langley Park. It was an undisputed success and all profits went to the Bromley branch of the *Alzheimer's Disease Society*.

Tim Pearce (left), Vicky Pearce and Steve Williams in The Taming of the Shrew *presented by* The Matchbox Theatre *in 1998*
Photo: Captured Images

The Normanhurst Festival was staged again in 1996 – featuring *Twelfth Night* and excerpts from *Trial by Jury* and *Madam Butterfly* by *Kentish Opera* – and in 1998 with *The Taming of the Shrew* and *Iolanthe* by *Kentish Opera*. It raised almost £9,000 for *Bromley Mencap Blue Sky Appeal* and was attended by *Mencap*'s chairman Sir Brian Rix. The next Festival is in 2000.

The society presents three plays a year but doesn't enter Guild festivals as yet.

Fiddler

The Guild followed up *Oliver!* with another blockbuster West End musical for its 1981 production – *Fiddler on the Roof*. Jeffrey Smith was back in the producer's seat and Robert Long once again responsible for the musical direction.

The 'fiddler' of the title was schoolboy actor Michael Hughes whose job it was to open the show by playing its plaintive theme tune perched high on one of the sets.

'It's pretty tricky playing up there – especially as the set moves while I'm playing', he said at the time. 'There's a special brace to keep me steady, though, so I should be alright'.

Michael's roof was just one of the mobile sets designed by Sally Langford (better known as director of *Kentish Opera*) which rolled into 22 different positions to provide varying backgrounds.

Stage adaptation of TV play

Robin Redbreast – John Bowen's unsettling play about a pagan fertility ritual in a modern setting – was the Guild's rather brave 1982 offering directed by William Burford at *Bromley Little Theatre*'s headquarters.

Written for television and first broadcast in 1971, its impact was such that it was repeated six weeks later owing to public demand. The problem with adapting it for the stage was how to cope with all those short, punchy scene-changes that work so effectively on the small screen.

Undeterred, Burford resorted to frequent blackouts and if, ultimately, the Bromley audiences didn't quite get the full impact enjoyed by television viewers they certainly left the theatre disturbed by his interpretation.

I found David Evans' 'reading' of the enigmatic Rob (the 'sacrificial bull' as Keith Lancing in the *Advertiser* described his character) particularly telling and the production was lent considerable weight by an imaginative cutaway set by Jill Burford.

Death of Allan Holliday

Allan Holliday's death in 1983 was a huge loss to the Guild. Without his energy the idea might never have got off the ground and since its inception he had held almost every Guild office.

It was also a personal sadness for me. I had

lost a good friend – a diplomatic and caring Editor-in-Chief in my early years as a journalist and latterly, a highly-valued contributor to the *Kentish Times* arts pages after his retirement.

Allan Holliday

(Our jolly 'phone conversations used to brighten the day considerably.)

In the June following Allan Holliday's death the Guild staged *The Canterbury Tales* at Bromley Civic Centre – not an ideal venue as producer Ray Harris can confirm. (Harris had staged a hugely successful version for his own society – *Theatre 62* – in 1979 when 'inventiveness and ingenuity' were the key words of this ambitious venture).

'At the time the council was still trying to make the performance space viable as a "theatre" and we encountered all sorts of practical problems – particularly setting up the lighting. However, artistically it was good and had a strong cast – including Terry Gauntlett and his son Richard – now professional'.

Musical director was Dave Pestell and the choreography was by Judy Frisby and Sue Hann.

Decadent

Jeffrey Smith was asked to produce the Guild's 1984 show – the persuasively decadent *Cabaret* (strangely at odds with its venue – Orpington Civic Hall, I remember it struck me at the time!). Audiences were seated at individual tables with waiter service in an attempt to create an authentic atmosphere.

Alain Smith choreographed the production and Dave Pestell was musical director of this powerful and evocative musical set in pre-Third Reich Germany and based on John Van Druten's *I Am A*

Camera and stories by Christopher Isherwood.

It's a tough nut to crack for an amateur group but this one acquitted itself well enough.

Briar Blake (Fraulein Schneider) recalls a 'frantic lurch to the first night against all odds following cancelled rehearsals; manic get-togethers in Jeffrey Smith's front room in Locksbottom; last-minute changes to the schedule and dashing off to Pratts Bottom for costume fittings!'

But 'despite all that, great friendships were forged that are still going strong 15 years later'.

Ron Mackay's death

In 1985 – just two years after Allan Holliday's death – Ron Mackay, the Guild's popular and hard-working secretary of 13 years, finally lost his battle against illness. It was another blow for the Guild and a time for reflection in a year that had also brought a fresh chapter in the continuing saga of the longed-for amateur theatre.

In buoyant mood, Stan Mole had announced in the press that the Guild was launching a £500,000 appeal in the hope of financing a theatre that would 'help make the borough the major centre for the arts outside the West End'. It was to be named after the Bromley playwright Lord Ted Willis and the aim was to raise the cash by early 1986.

He reminded the community in general (and the Guild in particular) that when the Guild was formed in 1949 plans were already in the pipeline to build a theatre. Many other areas smaller than Bromley had managed to build their own guild theatre, he said.

In 1987 he was to resign as chairman – still no nearer his dream.

A lavish production of *My Fair Lady* booked at the *Churchill Theatre* in 1986 was cancelled at an advanced stage because of lack of support (despite a membership of 36 societies) but in 1987 the Guild teamed up with *Bromley Ecumenical Parish* and *Bromley Arts Council* for *The Nativity*.

The play was part of the *Cycle of Mystery Plays* by Tony Harrison and the company – calling itself the *Beta Players* – was directed by Robert Dilks. The production scored a hit, Donald Madgwick going overboard on Brian McEwan's 'lip-smacking, roaring Herod' who made the performance 'crackle like flames sweeping through dry tinder' and Arthur Rochester's 'jealous God attired in cloth cap, belt and braces and speaking with reassuring northern vowels'.

The 'galloping alliteration' made for a boisterous effect and the music – played and sung by the *Beta Band* under the direction of Ian Skipper – was 'often magnificent in its impact'.

Madgwick doesn't mention the backstage team (I think he ran out of space) but I see that Barbara Sowerbutts was choreographer and Annie McAlister was in charge of costumes.

No show for three years

It was three years before the Guild staged another show – its last, as it turned out. In the meantime Robert Dilks had succeeded Stan Mole as chairman and in turn stepped down for Steve Williams (in 1988).

Arthur Rochester, Simon Whitelocke and Ivor Kemp in the Guild's production of The Nativity *in 1987*

The Festival of Arts for Bromley Borough in 1990 was the spur the Guild needed. As it was the centenary of Agatha Christie's birth, it was decided to revive *Witness for the Prosecution*. If somewhat dated (the film version always fares better than the stage adaptation) it was, nonetheless, an ideal showcase for the Guild, providing excellent acting opportunities which in the main were in very efficient hands under the direction of Roger Chinn.

Both the *Advertiser* and *Kentish Times* critics were of one mind over the impressive characterisations of Arthur Rochester (Sir Wilfred); Ronald Merrett (Meyers); Ray Harris (the judge) and Edna Walker (the housekeeper) but clearly at odds with each other over the playing of Romaine (Lynda Goddard) and Leonard Vole (Steve Williams) – which only goes to show what actors have always believed about critics...

Kathy Silk (the court stenographer) was in charge of wardrobe for the production.

(Documentation for some of the later Guild shows is thin on the ground hence the omission of photographs and other information for some years.)

Competitive festivals

Competitive drama festivals have long been a part of the amateur theatre scene throughout the country and as early as 1952 the Guild's member societies were entering their productions for the

Arthur Rochester (left); Steve Williams (centre) and Bill Walker in Witness for the Prosecution *presented by the Guild in 1990*
Photograph: Edward Harris

annual *Kent Festival*.

For the benefit of those readers who are not familiar with the procedure, it entails a qualified adjudicator (usually a member of the Guild of Drama Adjudicators) watching each entry – often as many as 30 or more! – at its own venue and giving a public assessment after the performance. Entries are judged under various headings:

production, acting, presentation and the somewhat enigmatic combination of 'endeavour, originality and attainment'.

The adjudicator then allocates marks under each of the headings and an overall percentage score to each society. The three highest-scoring societies are invited to stage their entries at Maidstone's *Hazlitt Theatre* for a final winner.

Several Guild members continue to enter the Kent Festival and have achieved a number of 'Final' appearances.

New proposal

Between 1952 and 1977 the marks awarded to Guild societies taking part in the Kent Festival were used to decide a Bromley winner as well as various other Bromley awards. At the Guild's AGM in 1977 it was decided to set up a new Festival – the *Bromley Full Length Play Festival* – to be run on similar lines but without a separate final round.

Since then, competing societies have been invited to Wickham Theatre Centre, *Theatre 62*'s home, when the adjudicator summarises his or her public adjudications, announces the results and presents the awards.

The first new-look festival was held in 1978 with 12 entries adjudicated by the late Duncan Rand. The *Josiah Merrill Shield* for Best Production went to Crayford's *Geoffrey Whitworth Theatre* (not a Guild member) for *Major Barbara* and runner up was *Hayes Players* with *Absurd Person Singular*. Best Producer was Elizabeth Finch (*Hayes Players*) and other acting prizes went to the *Geoffrey Whitworth Theatre*, *Hayes Players*, *Burnt Ash Drama Association* and *Farnborough* and *St Luke's* dramatic societies.

Apart from 1990 when the Guild's production of Agatha Christie's *Witness for the Prosecution* was staged at the *Churchill Theatre* as part of the *Festival of the Arts for Bromley Borough*, the Festival has been held annually and winners of the best productions include:

1979 *Geoffrey Whitworth Theatre* with *Florence Nightingale*

1980 *Burnt Ash Drama Association* with *Ghosts*

1981 *Burnt Ash Drama Assocation* with *The Long and the Short and the Tall*

1982 *Theatre 62* with *The Diary of Anne Frank*

1983 *Burnt Ash Drama Association* with *Enter a Free Man*

1984 *Theatre 62* with *Our Town*

1985 *Whitfield Players* with *Flowering Cherry*

1986 *Theatre 62* with *Dark of the Moon*

1987 *Theatre 62* with *The Cherry Orchard*

1988 *Geoffrey Whitworth Theatre* with *Ghosts*

1989 *Theatre 62* with *Cider With Rosie*

1991 *Burnt Ash Drama Association* with *Molly*

1992 *Orpington Amateur Repertory Club* with *Daisy Pulls It Off*

1993 *Theatre 62* with *A Voyage Round My Father*

1994 *Orpington Amateur Repertory Club* with *The Odd Couple*

1995 *Bromley Little Theatre* with *Our Country's Good*

1996 *New Wickham Court Players* with *The Glass Menagerie*

1997 *Pratts Bottom Dramatic Society* with *Farndale Avenue Macbeth*

1998 *Burnt Ash Drama Association* with *Night of the Iguana*

Today the Festival is the principal – in fact almost the only – joint enterprise of the Guild and the final adjudication is an enjoyable gathering of 'the family'.

Donald Madgwick used to relish the chance of attending the final adjudication night of the Festival.

'This is the big one – the night when friends and rivals foregather; where the best and the bravest of the various societies meet to learn the result of all the honest endeavour of the preceding months.

'There is always a great spirit of camaraderie between the constituent groups, the cream of which until comparatively recently were brought together for the now extinct combined Guild productions'.

Awards increased

The range of individual and group awards has steadily increased and the current 15 have mostly been presented by – or in memory of – former Guild luminaries such as Joe Merrill, Barbara Barnes, Sylvia Love, Ralph Allen, Dorothy Marriott, Allan Holliday, Ray Bardell, Ron Mackay, Robin Waldron and, more recently, Anne Curnow.

From the start, adjudicators' fees and other costs have been met by a grant from Bromley Arts Council – to which the Guild is indebted for its continuing support – but member societies now have to pay an additional small entrance fee.

Attitudes towards a competitive Festival differ among the Guild. There are those who, for their own reasons, have never entered. The societies who do participate – about nine or 10 – appear to feel that the event contributes significantly to meeting one of the Guild's key aims: the raising of artistic standards in the borough.

Attempt to bring societies closer together

A former chairman of the Guild, Steve Williams feels that it's the competitive nature of the Festivals that alienates some societies.

In 1992 – in an attempt to bring members closer together again – he decided to reinstate the one act play festival.

'I thought it would be a much bigger incentive if we dispensed with awards and adjudications and organise it so that each society got a percentage of the number of tickets they sold'.

Single-minded and determined it would succeed, Williams organised the event meticulously, 'bullying' people into taking part; writing letters to potential advertisers; arranging the programme and tackling the pile of administrative tasks. It was a mammoth commitment, taking a year to complete, but a rewarding one – particularly when it came to the moment when the committee allocated the profits of the 1993 festival to the participating societies.

'I was proud. It was nice to be able to sit back at the end of it all and find that the event had earned far in excess of what I'd imagined'.

Williams, for the most part, organised the 1994 festival but by this time his work commitments forced him to resign as chairman. After the 1995 festival no-one had the necessary time to invest in the project. Whether anyone will in the future remains to be seen.

On the subject of the future, Williams mentions words like 'insular' and 'parochial', saying that unless societies are more open with each other and 'share' their members, the Guild will die.

'Actors should be able to float between societies. I know there are concerns about this in case a society loses some of its best people but that doesn't have to happen. *The Matchbox* has opened a lot of eyes in this respect by bringing people in from other groups for its productions. The only way forward is for everyone to get something out of the Guild'.

The word for survival, then – and assuming that members want the Guild's survival – is sharing. But it's not just about sharing resources. It means being prepared to share ideas in an increasingly competitive arena.

While writing the closing chapter of the book I learned that the Guild has recently welcomed another society into the fold – the *Phoenix Drama Group* of Petts Wood.

Created out of the now extinct Lynwood Players, the group presents two productions a year and attracts members of all age groups.

Understandably, the latest addition to the 'family' brings a sense of new beginnings and a stronger belief in a future.

Index

figures in **bold** type indicate an illustration

A

Actories, The 69, 71
Allen, Ralph 20, 21, 56, 59, 79, 99
And So To Bed 21, 50–1, **50**
Ann Veronica **77**, 78
Aperfield Players 4, 64
Atkins, Robert 9, **9**, 19
Ayckbourn, Alan vi

B

Beckenham Advertiser 19, 59, 64, 75, 79, 81, 83, 84, 87, 93, 96
Beckenham Amateur Dramatic Society (BADS) v, 13–16, **14**, **15**, 25, 81
Beckenham Children's Theatre 14–15
Beckenham Festival of Original One Act Plays 15
Beckenham Journal 8, 14, 19, 51, 56
Beckenham Theatre Centre 14–5, 81
Bequest to the Nation 73, 87, **88**
Boleyn Players 73
Bromley Arts Council 78, 79, 95, 99
Bromley Borough Arts Festival 85, 96, 98
Bromley Full Length Play Festival 10, 14, 16, 24, 27, 33, 34, 36, 39, 42, 56, 60, 61, 67, 69, 70, 98–100
Bromley Home Guard Association Dramatic Society 4, 31
Bromley & Kentish Times 3, 8, 19, 47, 51
Bromley Little Theatre (BLT) 11, 25–7, **27**, **28**, **29**, 93, 99
Bromley Mercury 19
Bromley One Act Play Festival 20, 23, 50
Bromley Players 4, 36, 46–9 **46**, **48**, **49**, 56
Burford, William 67, 83, 87, 93
Burns, Doris 56
Burnt Ash Drama Association (BADA) 64–9, **66**, **68**, 70, 85, 86, 98, 99
see also St Andrew's Drama Association

C

Cabaret 94–5,
Canterbury Tales, The 94
Cat Among the Pigeons 84, **85**
Cavalcade 10, 81, 82, **82**
Chelsfield Players, The 25, 34–6, **34**, **35**
Chinn, Roger 96
Churchill Theatre, The v, 34, 85, 95, 98
Churchill Theatre Youth Section (CYTS) 67, 84–6, **86**

Cockett, Amy 4–6, 9, 20, 22, 23, 24, 25, 64, 78, 81
Cockett, Jack 4–6, 9, 20, 23, 24, 25, 50, 56
Coombs, Pat 43
Costume Bureau 9–10
Cronk, Margaret 9–10, 81, 87
Croydon Advertiser 54, 60

D

Dark of the Moon 82–3
Denham, Maurice 13

E

Edwardians, The 79–80, **80**
Eltham Little Theatre 83
Evening News, The 17, 41

F

Farnborough Dramatic Society (FDS) 36–9, **37**, **38**, 98
Festival *see* Bromley Full Length Play Festival, Bromley One Act Play Festival, Bromley Borough Arts Festival
Fiddler on the Roof 93
Finch, Graham 34, 89
Frisby, Beryl 17–18, 19, 56

G

Gass, Norman 4, 8, 9, **9**, 17, 18, 19, 21
Gay Lord Quex, The 20
Glebe Knoll Players 23, 59
Green Room, The 10
Green Room Club 23, 56
Guildmore Players, The 4

H

Hahlo, Peter 81
Hampton, H.B. v, 20, 59, 60
Hanff, Helene 61–3
Harris, Ray 48, 73, 77–8, 83, 87, 90, 94, 96
Harris, Rosemary 47, 73, 75, 77, 78, 87, 90
Hayes Players 4, 10, 20, 25, 31–4, **32**, **33**, 70, 79, 92, 98
Holliday, Allan v, 3, 8, 19, 23, 51, 79, 89, 93–4, **94**, 99
Holy Trinity Convent Dramatic Society 4
Hudd, Roy 10, 43
Hurst, John 16, 81
Hyams, Elisabeth 79, 87

I

Importance of Being Earnest, The 9, 64, **65**

J

Janes, Jane 9, 81, 83
Jason, David 36
Jones, W. Morgan 59

K

Kentish Opera 93
Kentish Times v, 6, 8, 10, 14, 20, 21, 59, 60, 64, 78, 82, 83, 94, 96
Kentish Times Critics' Award 10
Keston Amateur Dramatic Society 4, **53**, 54
see also *St Mark's & Keston Players*
Kismet Players 73

L

Lewis, Martin 13
Locke, Dorothy 83–4, 90

M

McCarthy, Darryl 10–11
Mackay, Ron 34, 95, 99
Macmillan, Harold 59
Madgwick, Donald 54, 75, 81, 83, 84, 86, 95
Marlowe Society 83
Marriott, Dorothy 79, 89, 99
Matchbox Theatre, The 90–3, **91**, **92**, 100
Matthew, Brian 36
Maunder, Frank 4, 60
Merlin Players 4
Merrill, Joe 20, 31, 59, 99
Merril Shield 20, 23, 98
Midsummer Night's Dream, A 4–9, **5**, **6**, **7**, **12**, 20
Minack Theatre 67, **68**, 70, 71
Mole, Stan 10, 80–1, 89, 90, 95, 96
Morant, Stephen 82, 86

N

National Operatic and Dramatic Association (NODA) 85
Nativity, The 95, **96**
New Theatre 16, 18, 20, 23, 50, 56, 59, 64, 79, 81
New Wickham Court Players 73, 99
see also *Wickham Court Players*
North West Kent Federation of Townswomen's Guilds 83

O

Oliver! 90, 93
Orpington Amateur Repertory Club (OARC) 36, 39–42, **40**, **42**, 98, 99

P

Paice, Margaret 18, 22, 23, 59
Pett, John 59–60
Phoenix Drama Group 100
Pomander Walk 17–20, **18**, **19**, 21, 56
Pratts Bottom Dramatic Society 99

Q

Quavers 4

R

Rada Players, The 4
Raffaleans 13

Rape of the Belt, The 75–7, **76**
Regents Park Open Air Theatre 9
Ridley, Ken 3, 20
Ring Round the Moon 59
Ripley Arts Centre 81, 90
Robin Redbreast 93
Rochester, Arthur 1, 64, 87, 90, 95, 96
Russell, Cliff v, 47, 79, 83, 89

S

St Andrew's Dramatic Society 64, 67, **66**, 69
  see also Burnt Ash Drama Association
St Luke's Amateur Dramatic Society (SLADS) 4, 18, 22–5, **24**, **26**, 36, 98
St Mark's & Keston Players 54–5, **55**
  see also St Mark's Players and *Keston Amateur Dramatic Society*
St Mark's Players 51–4, **52**, 83
  see also St Mark's & Keston Players
Scott, Katheryn 78
Smith, Audrey 59, 64, 75, 78
Smith, Jeffrey 90, 93, 94, 95
Swift 10, The 4

T

Theatre 62 10, 67, 69–73, **71**, **72**, 94, 98, 99
Thornton, Victor v, 8, 14, 19
Times Educational Supplement, The 9
Tinker, Ron 83, 84
Tom Jones 36, 83–4, **84**
Trial of Mary Dugan, The 56–7, **57**
Twelfth Night 20, 21, **22**, 83

V

Verney, Guy 18, 20
Vivat! Vivat! Regina! 86–7

W

Waldron, Robin 20, 21–2, 99
Waldron Shield 20, 23
Walker, Edna 37, 38, 83, 84, 87, 96
Waltz of the Toreadors, The **75**, 77
West Wickham Amateur Dramatic Society 4, 69, 73
West Wickham Operatic Society (WWOS) 73
West Wickham Pantomime Society (WWPS) 36, 43–5, **44**, **45**
West Wickham Theatre Guild 73
When We Are Married 59
Whitfield Players 60–4, **61**, **63**, 67, 98
Wickham Court Players 4, 73
  see also New Wickham Court Players
Williams, Gerald 4, 20, 79, 83
Williams, Steve 34, 64, 96, 99–100
Witness for the Prosecution 34, 96, **97**, 98

Y

York, Michael 26–7

Endnote

Inevitably, there will be names who do not appear in the book. No slight is intended on the part of the author who did her best to include as many as space (and contributed information) would permit.

Thanks are due to Audrey Smithard for proof reading the book.

Every effort has been made to source and credit photographs.